The New Teacher's Guide:

*A New(ish) Teacher's Honest Advice
for Better Classroom Management*

ALISA L. SWAIN

authorHOUSE®

AuthorHouse™
1663 Liberty Drive
Bloomington, IN 47403
www.authorhouse.com
Phone: 1 (800) 839-8640

Published by AuthorHouse 03/23/2018

ISBN: 978-1-5462-3355-8 (sc)
ISBN: 978-1-5462-3353-4 (hc)
ISBN: 978-1-5462-3354-1 (e)

Library of Congress Control Number: 2018903381

For Mama, Thank you for always supporting my dreams no matter how BIG they get.

Contents

If you're picking up this book, you are probably a new teacher, and I bet I know a little something about how you might be feeling: Tired, because the school day starts early and lesson planning runs late, especially in those early years when you're starting from scratch. Overwhelmed, because every day you take on innumerable tasks and constant decision-making. Broke, because teacher pay is—let's face it—not great, and student loans loom large, not to mention all the classroom supplies that come from your own paycheck because you want your students to have the resources they need to succeed.

And yet, despite all these feelings, I bet if you're picking up this book, you're still really excited and eager to be a teacher. You care. Plain and simple. If you didn't care, my words wouldn't be in your hands right now. You care, and you want to be the best teacher you can possibly be. If you're like me, you believe that teaching is a calling, not just a career. It's a vocation that can move mountains, change the world, and enrich countless lives, including your own. And you have faith that it will get better than the struggles of these early years. And I'm here to say, it can and it *will*, and I'm here to help.

Who am I?

Well, I'm Alisa to you, my readers, Ms. Swain to my students, and as I write these words, a seven-year teacher of middle school Language Arts in the Georgia public school system.

Now, you may be wondering why you should bother reading a book by a teacher with only seven years' experience under her belt instead of hunting down sage advice from veteran educators who have spent decades in the classroom. By all means, read those books, too!

But this one holds something more for you, something special and just for you, the new teacher. My perspective is unique and my position is, in my humble opinion, invaluable right now, which is why despite the many demands on my time and attention, I feel compelled to write this book *now*, before more experience changes my perspective. I recognize that I am uniquely positioned: I've been where you are—the steep learning curve, the self-doubt, the desperate need for real, practical solutions that will actually help—but I'm not there anymore, thank goodness (at least, not on most days). But I also don't have decades of experience clouding my very vivid memories of what those early years were like. I know how real and emotional and taxing the new-teacher struggle is. I remember it well. Believe me; my rose-colored glasses have not come in yet!

So this book is my hard-won, honest advice to new teachers, the things I wish I had known in my first days about how to manage a classroom effectively, boiled down to simple strategies that you can start putting into practice tomorrow to see real results. I know you don't have a lot of time on your hands, so this book is concise and easily skimmable. You can read it cover-to-cover in just a few hours and then, in years to come when you're no longer a new teacher, you can return to it again and again, any time you need quick inspiration or a refresher on how to get the most out of your classroom management.

Why Classroom Management?

Every year, I feel like I observe the same thing—despite all the varied demands that are put on teachers, the thing that most causes them to walk away from the profession is an inability to manage their classrooms and student behaviors. My school, like many others, seems to have a new educational approach to implement every year, some brand-new strategy for raising test scores and improving student achievement. But whatever the latest education fad, the common denominator for it all to be successful is that the students have to be cooperative. I have seen so many teachers become discouraged along the way, largely because the challenge of classroom management just seems so insurmountable. They give up not only on the students they teach, but on themselves as teachers.

The sad reality is that many teachers do not make it past their third year. New teachers find themselves equipped with a degree that they cannot use and student loan debts that they can no longer afford to pay back, and they feel exhausted just trying to make it through each day. Trust me; I have been on the verge of quitting many times, wondering if it's all worth it. But it *can* get better, with practice and patience and the classroom management strategies I outline in this book. I share these strategies with you so that you can make it past year three. Our children need us—teachers who care—to stick around. They need caring teachers like you to inspire them and build them up so that they can become great people who, like you, go out and change the world in positive and lasting ways.

"I am always fine until the kids come."

One day in my first year of teaching, I was talking with another new teacher. We were venting our frustrations over all the new challenges we were facing and she said, "I am always fine until the kids come." We laughed it off, but the reality is, many new teachers feel this way. We feel great about teaching until we're faced with the actual challenges of classroom management. We feel confident and comfortable with our positions until that moment our students walk through our doors. Because the children are the ones who demand our best and help us see if we are really prepared.

This book will teach you how to embrace a perspective where you see your students not as the most difficult part of your day, but as the inspiration and catalyst behind your growth as a teacher and, honestly, as a person. Your students and their impact on your life will become some of the biggest rewards of your career.

Lessons from Both Sides of the Desk

No matter where you are in your career as a new teacher—whether you've just graduated with your degree (if so, congratulations) or you've had a handful of years in the classroom—there will be days when you think, "I have no idea what I'm doing! I don't know how to handle this!" Take comfort in the fact that we've all been there. Then take a moment and close your eyes. Think about your educational experiences as a child. Who was your favorite teacher? Why was this person your favorite? Think back to the worst teacher you ever had. What made him or her so bad?

Like anything else, who you are as a teacher has been influenced by your experiences in education already. When you struggle with classroom management, stop and take time to reflect on who you want to be as a teacher based on your past experiences and the teachers who had the most impact on you. Children today deal with challenges greater than some of us can even imagine, but they are still just children. They consider their likes and dislikes for teachers in many of the same ways we did. It is important to establish what kind of teacher you want to be so that you always have that goal in mind. Reflecting on your past—the experiences that shaped you, the teachers you loved, the teachers you hated—will help you see that you already have inside you the framework for being a great teacher.

Throughout this book, I share with you my own such reflections. I recount stories from my childhood, memories of either positive or negative experiences from my K-12 education that have helped mold me into the teacher I am today. I also share many teaching experience stories as well, because every teacher should take the time to reflect on what happens in the classroom—the good, the bad, and the ugly. Together, my old and new memories give you two perspectives on many of the same classroom management topics.

My hope is that my stories will not only entertain you but also spark reflection on your part. What similar experiences have you had? How have they shaped you? What have you learned? This book is designed to both tell you my story and encourage you to discover yours. Although you may have never been a teacher before, you have been a student. The beauty of this profession is that everyone who enters it has already been on the other side of the desk. Think back to that student. What did younger you love about school? What did you hate? Work from that point. Listen to that student and become the teacher your inner student would be proud of.

Strategy #1:

Build Trust

The Poem

As I stood there awkwardly at her desk, waiting for her to finish reading my poem, I couldn't help but think, "Am I doing the right thing? Should I have allowed her to read my real feelings?"

My hands were starting to glisten with sweat. I rubbed them on my pant legs to absorb some of the moisture. I wanted to look at her, but I was afraid that her face would show displeasure.

Look away. No, look.

I slowly looked up at Mrs. Penny.[1] There were tears in her eyes. She quickly brushed them away and whispered, "It's lovely, Alisa."

"Thank you," I whispered back.

We exchanged soft smiles, and I placed my poem back in my folder and walked out of the room.

I had done it. I had shared my poem with Mrs. Penny, and she had liked it.

Mrs. Penny was my 7th grade teacher, and she had given our class an assignment to write a poem about someone who was important to us, and I had chosen to write about my father. He passed away when I was only eight years old, so discussing him was a touchy subject for me. But somehow I had known that this assignment was an important opportunity to express some of the feelings I had about him and his death.

I remember that day I was proud of my work, but I was too scared to share it in front of the class like everyone

---

[1] All names, aside from my own, have been changed to ensure privacy.

else. Without judgment, Mrs. Penny had agreed to read it privately once class was over.

Her simple, affirming words, "It's lovely," combined with her gentle spirit and sincere emotion gave me the reassurance I needed. From that moment on, I understood that I could trust her with my work and with my feelings. Her brief yet meaningful response helped me to become more open—open to a more trusting and fulfilling relationship with her, my teacher, but also open to a bit of healing from my loss and grief. Mrs. Penny gave me an invaluable gift that day, one that I continue to cherish.

Trust is where it all starts. If you don't start there, any other efforts you make to control your classroom will eventually fail.

It's something we are often evaluated on—whether we have established a positive classroom environment. Do our students feel safe to ask questions and make comments without ridicule or judgment? Do they feel that we listen to them and really hear what they have to say? Are they welcomed into our classrooms each day and valued as an important part of our classroom community? Can they trust that we, their teachers, will do what we say we will do and that we will hold them accountable for their own actions and behaviors?

"Effective, long-term classroom management is built on a solid foundation of trust between you and your students."

As a teacher, it is your job to make sure that each of your students feels comfortable in your class. You want to be the very first person at your school that your students trust. So how do you do that, establish trust? How do you go from the first day of school when everyone is a stranger to the last day when your students are sad to leave because of the community you have built together?

In this chapter, I explore a number of ways to foster this kind of authentic trust. These strategies are often so simple and easy, and simultaneously so powerful. You can start doing them tomorrow and will begin to see changes in your classroom culture almost immediately.

Smile

Smile. Yes, it is just that simple. Smile, and smile often. It is so easy to do, and yet I have found that so many teachers either forget this simple strategy or, more likely, are afraid to smile because they have the misconception that smiling is a sign of weakness to their students.

Let me assure you, smiling does not cause you to lose control of your class; in fact, it can actually help you gain *more* control. My students not only understand my verbal cues but also my nonverbal ones. Smiling when you are happy or enjoying the class and the lesson will allow your students to pick up on when you are unhappy with their behaviors. When a teacher who often smiles during his or her lessons suddenly starts frowning, students realize very quickly that something is not right. Without your having to say a word, they will understand that things are out of place and something needs to change. Of course, there will be times when you must verbally address the negative behaviors, but eventually your students will recognize the pattern and simple, nonverbal cues, like a frown, will allow you to correct the problem without disrupting your lesson.

Smiling also puts your students at ease. If you are constantly scowling at them, they will not feel comfortable in your classroom. Students are able to pick up on the energy of their teachers. You want your students to be happy and excited about learning. Remember that your energy will dictate the direction of the classroom energy. If you discover that you're not smiling at your students because you are too exhausted and overwhelmed (I've been there), pause here and turn to Strategy #5 on self-care. It is extremely difficult to be upbeat and approachable when you are stressed and run down. Taking good care of yourself will go a long way toward better classroom management—and you'll find that you smile more in other parts of your life, too!

Speak to Everyone

Speaking to everyone is important because many students who are quiet or rarely in trouble can start to feel that they are invisible in class. If teachers mainly interact with the students who exhibit behavior problems, then others may begin to develop similar negative behaviors just to get the attention they crave. Always make sure that each student feels that he or she is a vital member of the group. There are a number of simple ways you can provide this kind of positive attention to each and every one of your students.

If you are a middle school or high school teacher, the time when your students are changing classes is a perfect opportunity to speak to them all as they enter your classroom. Some of your students who are very shy and reserved may never speak to you during class, but this transitional time during the day is your chance to make a connection.

Before each class period, I stand and greet my students as they enter my room. In addition to establishing a warm tone with them, this greeting gives me a gauge on how they may be feeling that day. Some students enter bubbly and full of life. They are excited and happy to be at school again. Others may barely respond when I say hello. I also pay close attention to their body language. If a student is not looking at me or speaks very softly, then I know to look out for that student. Watching the soft-spoken and reserved students can help you see if they are just shy or if perhaps there is something going on at home that you need to report.

Another way to connect with students is during independent work. Walk around and assist while students are working on their own. I try to speak to students who do not open up much during group or whole class discussions. I spend a little extra time at their desks to make sure they do not feel left out or overlooked.

Down time is another great time to make a connection. Students often complete independent assignments at different times, allowing those who finish early the opportunity to read or work on something else while they wait for everyone to finish. Walk around during this time and strike up a conversation about what you see. Comment on Sally's book. Give Jamal a compliment on his drawing. All of these interactions give students an opportunity to have some time with you one-on-one, which makes them feel valued.

Just be sure that all of your greetings, comments, and compliments are genuine. Students can tell rather quickly when a teacher is just trying to be nice but doesn't really care. Coming off as disingenuous can be just as harmful as not speaking to students at all. When students become comfortable with you and see that you are sincere and approachable, they will be more likely to care about your class and follow your directions.

Stop the Buses

Every year I always have an extremely shy child in my classroom. This particular year was no different. Maria was my shy girl. You could look into her large brown eyes and tell that life for her had already been difficult. She would give me a slight smile each morning, but her slow shuffle into my classroom with her hair covering most of her face told a different story. She did not talk loudly about boys like the other girls, their voices soaring over my lessons like a gospel choir, everyone with a different part but all in harmony. Maria was not active like the boys, bouncing from seat to seat, always looking for a reason to get up.

No, Maria was different. She sat in her seat every day, listening intently through the chaos. When I saw her, I always smiled. Maria was not a strong writer; she often stayed after class to ask me to review her work. I always took some time to read her papers and give her feedback for improvement.

As the year progressed, Maria began to become even more withdrawn. Her slumped shoulders almost created a hump in her back. I imagined her bending so far over in hopes of becoming invisible. But I saw her. I always tried to find time to speak to Maria. I never inquired about why she was so sad or why she missed so many days of school, but instead I tried to focus on the beautiful drawings that she always doodled on the edges of her papers.

One day during bus call, Maria came up to me. The look in her eyes had changed. It was not one of hurt and shame but now one of urgency and fear. I stood up and moved closer to her so that no one could hear our conversation. She expressed to me that her friend Sarah was going to commit suicide when she got home from school.

The information startled me at first, but I recovered my composure quickly and hurried with Maria to the counselor's office, where Maria told her about Sarah's plan. The counselor called Sarah's parents and asked them to keep a close eye on her when she returned home.

Sarah didn't go through with it, and although Maria was so clearly dealing with her own demons, in that moment, she was selflessly looking out for a friend. I was so proud of her, and so thankful that she trusted me enough to confide something so serious.

The lesson I learned that day is that the trust we as teachers establish with our students can literally mean the difference between life and death. It may sound dramatic, but it's true, and building that trust happens with the small, everyday actions I'm offering in this book. You never know when a child will turn to you for help. All those extra hellos, those smiles, those kind words and moments when you show them that you care about what they care about—that you care about them—*all those little things lay the foundation for your relationship with them, building up their trust in you. A trust that may even save lives.*

Make Connections Outside the Classroom

It may take a little extra time and effort, but making connections with your students outside the classroom will go a long way toward easier classroom management. Try attending your students' sports games or practices. Take some time to watch a band performance or an orchestra concert. Students enjoy seeing their teachers at these events, supporting them in all aspects of their school life. When you show support of your students *outside* the classroom, you will notice a positive change in their behavior *inside* the classroom. Children crave support and acceptance, and they will be happy to know that you care.

If your schedule just does not allow you to attend your students' extracurricular activities, make it your responsibility to know when they have an event. Strike up a conversation with them about it the day after a performance or game. Students are pleased with this level of interest as well. Your ultimate goal is to make a connection and build a relationship with your students that will foster a productive learning environment.

Be a "Friendly Teacher"

When I first began teaching, I met a colleague who always told her students that she was their "friendly teacher" but not their friend. This distinction has always stuck with me. It is important to build relationships with students. In fact, it is the only way to run a smooth, positive learning environment. But it is also important to know the difference between being a friend and being a friendly teacher. Some teachers cross over this line without even being aware of it.

Avoid treating your students as if they were your peers. You should always treat them with respect, but keep in mind that you are the adult. Do not share too much of your personal business. Don't give students your personal telephone number or access to your social media accounts. Becoming too friendly with students will actually hurt your ability to manage the classroom. Students will no longer see you as their authority figure, because you will have become their "friend." They do not respect their friends in the same manner that they respect adults, so you will see a shift in their behavior should you become too friendly.

Know the Difference: Friend vs. Friendly Teacher

Friends...

- Tell each other everything.
- Talk outside of school.
- Are friends on social media.
- Talk about relationships and politics.
- Have equal say about what happens in the class.

Friendly teachers...

- Talk to students only about school-appropriate topics. Friendly teachers allow students to share their feelings about any issue, but they do not add personal views or biases.
- Know that there are limitations on what should be discussed with children.
- Talk to students only during the school day or at school-related events.
- Do not "friend" students on social media. Friendly teachers teach students that it is inappropriate for them to be friends online.
- Create their lessons in a way that allows for student choice; however, friendly teachers always make it clear that the final decision is theirs to make.

Panty Raids

My 5ᵗʰ grade teacher reminded me of Viola Swamp from the children's book Miss Nelson is Missing! *by Harry Allard and James Marshall. Like the fictional character, my real*

Viola Swamp was tall and thin with a very pointy nose. Her hair was as black as tar and her face was strikingly pale. She wore bright red lipstick, which she often paired with her regular outfit of a red turtleneck sweater and a long black skirt.

My Miss Swamp spent her mornings preparing her morning tea and meticulously applying her makeup in the locker mirror she attached to the inside of her cabinet door. She buzzed around the classroom greeting students but never preparing her actual lesson for the day.

Once class started, it was usually the same game: we waited for Miss Swamp to locate her reading glasses and her lesson. She often tried to tell us personal stories to help us remember what she was teaching. Even as a 5ᵗʰ grader, I was aware that her stories were highly inappropriate. She told us about her college days in the '70s when she participated in panty raids, which consisted of boys coming to the girls' dorm and demanding that they throw down their undergarments. How this story was supposed to help us remember the '70s, I'm not sure!

Miss Swamp was a very nice lady, but she was an awful teacher that year. It was obvious that she had no idea what she was doing. I didn't learn much 5ᵗʰ grade content, but I did learn the importance of avoiding "oversharing."

Share—But Don't Overshare

One common misconception in education is that we as teachers should not talk to our students about our personal lives. Now of course you want to stay within the confines of what is morally and ethically appropriate, but it is okay not to be a closed book. When greeting your students at the door, try asking them about their evening or weekend. If you have a common interest, this transitional part of your day is a great time to share it.

For example, a student may mention that their family went to the movies. If you too have seen that movie, then tell your student and have a brief conversation about what you both liked or disliked about it. This example may seem very basic, but students like to know that their teacher is a "real" person. They feel more comfortable talking to you and opening up if they believe that you are a real person with a real life and not just an impersonal transmitter of knowledge. Students who feel comfortable with their teachers are often willing to work harder for them as well as behave better.

It is also very important to share with students your flaws and shortcomings. I share with my students that I am not the greatest speller and that math is not my strength. This admission shows them that yes, I am their teacher, but I am not perfect. Students are more willing to try if they understand that everyone in the room (including you!) has an opportunity for growth and improvement. Some students come in feeling that they are the only ones who don't get it. Dispelling that defeated attitude early on can help you maintain good class participation and student effort levels. Set a culture in your classroom that helps everyone see an area for growth.

Don't Let Him Down

Kevin. I will always remember Kevin. He was a 6'2" 8th grader with as much anger as he had height. When Kevin was sweet, you didn't need a dessert at lunch. But when Kevin was angry, you needed the whole armor of God to place a hedge of protection around you. He loved being the center of attention and often forgot that it was my classroom and not his. But in spite of all that, I still really liked Kevin.

Of course, like many other young people who act out, Kevin had been through a lot. His father passed away when he was a young boy, and he was still dealing with his feelings about his father's death.

At the beginning of each school year, I always introduce myself and tell my new students a little bit about my family.

I sometimes share the fact that my father died when I was very young. I distinctly remember that after telling my story, Kevin whispered to me, "My father passed away, too." We gave each other that knowing look that only children of stolen moments can understand, and then I continued my walk through the rows of desks.

Kevin was never perfect for me because he was still dealing with his grief, but we had a connection that allowed him to never go too far. Whenever Kevin was in a place of rebellion, I would try to talk to him before he got out of control. Often I would remind him that he needed to do the right thing, that he should think about whether his actions would make his father proud.

Strategy #2:

Discipline Wisely

The Soggy Dorito

It was a typical afternoon with everyone sitting at their desks, busily working on their independent assignment. I decided to sit at my desk for a little while to take attendance and do some paperwork.

After a few moments, I began to scan the classroom to make sure all of my students were still on task. One student was up sharpening his pencil; the rhythmic crank of the sharpener was the only noise in the room. A row of students were intently focused on finishing their assignments, heads bent in concentration. One young man had already finished and was reading a Harry Potter book.

I noted these things, and then my eyes stopped on Ted. I observed that he was hovering close to his desk, his eyes full of guilt and fear. He looked left. He looked right. And then he took a chip out of the bag in his lap and ate it. He didn't notice that I was watching, so he went for another one. As he gorged on the second chip, our eyes met. He looked away quickly but still aware that I was there. He did not chew. He sat motionless, begging his peripheral vision to reveal that I was no longer looking his way. But I was. I purposely stopped what I was doing to see how long he was going to sit motionless without chewing or swallowing. I knew that there had to be at least two chips in his mouth getting soggier by the minute. He wouldn't dare chew or swallow because he knew that there was no eating in class. So there he was, trapped, his mouth a swamp of soggy Doritos.

After about three minutes, I resumed my inspection of the entire room. Ted was able to finish his slimy snack. He put the rest of the chips away undetected. I figured there was no need to give Ted a punishment. He had already suffered enough.

As a new teacher, what I needed most were some concrete strategies about how to manage my classroom. I often found myself in situations where things had gotten out of control and I had no idea how. This chapter offers my hard-won advice in the form of straightforward strategies that will help you avoid losing control of the learning environment. Your goal is, of course, to maintain control of your classroom; therefore, it is crucial that you teach your students your classroom procedures early on and help them understand your expectations from the start. That way, you can build up their trust in you and still hold them accountable for how they conduct themselves in your classroom. Remember that discipline is not a dirty word. Thoughtful discipline is an important way to make connections with your students. *Not* holding your students accountable when they break your rules sends the message that they cannot trust you at your word. When it comes to discipline, think of Dr. Seuss's *Horton Hatches the Egg*: "I meant what I said, and I said what I meant." The next line of the book is, "An elephant's faithful one-hundred percent." Be a faithful *teacher* and discipline your students with fairness and respect.

Control Yourself First

Before you can begin to control your classroom and manage your students' behaviors, you must first manage your own. Teaching is an emotional job. It can be simultaneously heartwarming and heartbreaking. As teachers, we witness horrible things about our students' home lives over which we have no control. We experience the very best and very worst behaviors they have to offer. We can be frustrated beyond reason as we try to manage hostile, defiant students, and many times we may want to scream or cry or both.

While all of these feelings are totally natural, it is crucial that you take your emotions out of classroom discipline. There is a time and place for dealing with your feelings, especially the difficult ones, but it is *not* in front of your students. You are their leader, their teacher. They need to be able to trust that you are in control, not just of your classroom, but of yourself. While it is great if they like you and enjoy swapping stories with you, the bottom line is that you want them to respect you and to feel that your classroom is a safe place to be, even (especially) when it comes to emotions, both theirs and yours.

So keep your cool. Do not allow students to see what angers you. Although you may allow them to see why your smile changes to a frown, you don't want them to see when your calm becomes frustration, anger, even rage. Remember to stay calm and use a soft voice. Some students are used to adults yelling at them when they become upset; don't be another one of those adults in their lives. The point is to maintain control. Some students may even look for your boiling point. I have witnessed students making a game of how long it would take to make a teacher angry or uncomfortable. These kinds of games and testing behaviors usually occur after a teacher has already slipped up and let students see him or her get upset. Don't fall into that trap. Controlling your emotions will help you stay in control of any classroom situation.

Don't Let It Slide/Let Some Stuff Go

There is a thin line between the "Don't let it slide" and "Let some stuff go" discipline philosophies. Teachers must walk this line *all day long*. We must decide which classroom behaviors require our immediate attention and which behaviors are best ignored. You will get better at making these judgment calls over time—and you will certainly get plenty of practice— but in the meantime, as a new teacher, you may find yourself wondering what to do when discipline problems arise, whether to let it go or to step in and take action. The following advice will help you make those calls.

"Don't let it slide" is a very important part of classroom management. In the first 60 days, you must set the tone for the year. Students are learning who you are by watching how you interact with the class. There is always at least one student who wants to test your classroom management. I call this student "the ringleader." This is the student who will be bold enough to be the first one in the class to act up. This student, as well as all the others, will be waiting to see your reaction to the misbehavior.

No matter what the offense may be, make sure that you address it. Depending on the offense, you may need to issue a consequence, but be sure to acknowledge the problem. If you do not directly address the first student who disrupts the class or talks back, you will be on the fast track to losing control of your classroom.

So how do you do this, address the problem? It depends entirely on the situation, but always remember that your goal is to maintain an environment conducive to learning. Choose a course of action that will minimize the disruption to your teaching while still holding the offending student accountable. My general rule is to start with the least intervention that you think will get the class back on track. Now, this may mean that you issue an immediate severe consequence if the misconduct warrants it, but my point is that you want to avoid over-disciplining when you "don't let it slide." Below I offer different discipline approaches in order of least intervention to greatest.

"Don't Let It Slide" Discipline Triage

Least intervention	Nonverbal redirection
	Verbal correction
	Private conference
	Written consequence
Most intervention	Administration involvement

Nonverbal Redirection

I often choose nonverbal redirection to address misbehaviors because it usually does not involve any of the other students. I give a nod, a look, a frown. Many times the rest of the class simply goes on working, unaware that I have redirected their classmate at all.

The "teacher face" is a great and highly effective nonverbal cue. Everyone is aware of the teacher face; it is that facial expression that you give to students to let them know that you mean business. Even if it feels awkward, be sure to practice your teacher face in the mirror before using it on a student. You want to make sure that it looks significantly different from your normal expressions. You also want to make sure that it conveys a sense of seriousness and urgency. Try asking friends or family to help you perfect your teacher face.

Other nonverbal cues work well when you do not want to disrupt the class by redirecting students out loud. I often use hand gestures (polite ones, of course) to instruct students to sit down, be quiet, or turn around. These misbehaviors are not things that I believe I must stop and address verbally, and I have found that most students will comply with nonverbal cues without any further instruction.

Verbal Correction

When you must say something aloud to your students to correct misbehavior, pay close attention to your tone of voice and volume. For example, the natural response to a loud room is for the person speaking to become even louder; however, it has been my experience that students do not respond well to a teacher who is screaming. Your need to raise your voice signifies your lack of control over the situation. It is important that you remain calm and in control when your students are not following directions. It is how you protect the trust your students place in you as their confident, capable leader.

So one way to maintain control is to avoid raising your voice. When students are speaking too loudly, try giving instructions in an even lower voice. Some students will notice that they cannot hear what you are saying, at which point you can explain that they did not hear you because the classroom is too loud. This awareness encourages those students to get quiet. What's more, you will often find that students will start to "police" each other, telling their disruptive classmates to quiet down so that they can hear you better.

Now of course, in some situations students are not going to pay attention if you don't get them quiet first. In this case, try using a call-and-response strategy. For example, I often say, very quietly, "If you can hear my voice, clap once," and then at least a few students clap. Then I say, "If you can hear my voice, clap twice," and then more students clap. I finish by saying, "If you can hear my voice, your voice is off." This call-and-response helps those students who are not paying attention to get on board and begin to focus their attention in the right direction. Remember, you do not yell these commands. Speak in a normal tone of voice. The students who are closest to you will start the response and the other students will soon follow.

Another great way to use voice volume to your advantage is when you are redirecting individual students. Avoid calling students out in front of the entire class. When students are disciplined in front of their peers, they often feel that they need to save face by being overly combative. In addition, speaking to students softly while they are seated at their desks will keep you from distracting the whole class when the redirection is only necessary for that individual student. Once again, the goal is to find the least disruptive way to correct the students who are misbehaving.

Personal Conference

A student who continues to act out or who disrupts the entire class needs more intervention. I usually ask a disruptive or defiant student to "step to the hall." Asking him or her to leave the classroom is a quick and effective way to get the lesson back on track, and it gives the student an opportunity to calm down. And in all honesty, it also gives that person a chance to "sweat" a little; the disruptive student is left in the hallway wondering what I am going to say or do next.

I allow students in this kind of "time out" to stay in the hall alone for 5-7 minutes, and then I go and conference with them. When conferencing with misbehaving students, I always start by asking them if they know why they were sent to the hall. Then I follow by reiterating my expectation for appropriate conduct in the classroom, and then I allow them to return to their desks.

I do *not* allow students to have much time to explain why they felt the need to act out. That is not the point of the conference. The point of the conference is to stop the disruption to the class and to have a discrete "mini lesson" with the misbehaving student about how to behave correctly. It is an important teaching moment, but it is not a prolonged conversation.

I *do* allow the offending students an opportunity to address the situation, because it is important to give them a voice and for them to feel heard. But I caution you that when you conference with your students, do not go back and forth with them. If they want to have a longer conversation about it with you, schedule it for another time. Below are some examples of how you might conference with disruptive students and how the conferences might go.

Compliant Student Conference

Teacher: Nicky, do you know why you were sent to the hall?

Nicky: Yes, I was yelling out while you were teaching.

Teacher: That's right, and you know that I will not tolerate your yelling in class. Now let's go back in. Have a seat and finish your assignment without talking.

Note how brief the teacher's comments are. She asserts her authority ("I will not tolerate...") and she reiterates the rule (no yelling in class), but then she moves on and immediately gets back to working with the entire class, effectively minimizing the disruption. The takeaway for effective discipline: Talk less. Teach more.

Defiant Student Conference

Teacher: John, do you know why you were sent to the hall?

John: No, I didn't even do anything. That was Teddy. You are always picking on me.

Teacher: John, I saw you out of your seat, hitting multiple students on the way back to your chair.

John: I only hit one person and he hit me first.

Teacher: John, you know that hitting is not allowed. You will serve silent lunch today for disrupting the class.

John: But it wasn't my fault—

Teacher: (Interjecting) I know you can make better choices in the future. Now let's go back inside so that you can finish your assignment.

In the defiant conference, John wanted to debate and provide excuses about his choice to misbehave. As the teacher, you want to minimize the student's opportunity to provide lengthy excuses. I try not to shut down the dialogue right away, because I don't want the child to think that his or her thoughts and opinions are not heard, but I also do not want students to think that offering an excuse will ever result in not having to take ownership of their actions.

It is important not to spend too much time in the hall, because you want to make sure that the rest of the class is not getting out of control while you are gone. Another way to avoid this situation would be to position yourself in a way that you can still see the students in the classroom. For example, there is a window in my classroom door, so I often stand where I can see inside and, equally important, the students can see me watching them. But make sure that the student you are conferencing with cannot be seen through the window. You do not want other students watching the conference. It undercuts the privacy of the moment and may be distracting as you try to get the defiant student to comply and take the conference seriously.

Again, the main point of the conference is to get the distraction out of the classroom. Even if students are combative, you want to state their reason for being in the hall and what your expectations are when they reenter your classroom. If at any time you feel that the conference is not going to change a disruptive child's behavior, then you may want to ask a colleague to allow the student to finish the period in his or her classroom. (See "Keep It in the Family" for more on this strategy.)

Of course, there is not always time for a conference in the hallway. An alternative to the hall conference is setting up an isolation area in your classroom. When a student is in need of a break from his or her peers, ask the disruptive student to sit in the isolation desk. This allows you to continue teaching while monitoring the misbehaving student at the same time. Once the class is working on something independently, then you can go over and conference quietly, just as you would in the hallway.

Also consider desk conferences. I call students up to my desk when they are off task during an independent assignment. You can have a conference with them at your desk similar to the hallway conference. Just be sure to lower your voice so that other students are not distracted by your conversation, and I often make desk conferences even shorter.

Desk Conference

Teacher: I see that you have not picked up your pencil. Do you plan on doing some work today?

Elena: Yes, I was just fixing my pencil.

Teacher: We have been working for ten minutes, (*handing Elena a pencil*) so get started.

Keeping the desk conference short helps minimize the distraction to other students. The point of the desk conference is to redirect the student quickly. Just the act of having to walk from their seat to your desk can be enough of a wakeup call for some students. Notice that in this example the teacher does not give Elena a consequence for being off task. Instead, she solves the problem and helps the student get back to work. Not every unwanted behavior requires a punishment.

Written Consequence and Administration Involvement

Nonverbal redirection, verbal correction, and private conferences are highly effective strategies for addressing 90% of the discipline problems you will encounter in the classroom. However, we all are aware of the other 10%—those student behaviors that must be documented with some form of paper consequence. A paper consequence can be any form of documentation for discipline. Most schools at any level have a referral process, which involves the teacher writing down the misbehaving student's actions and an administrator issuing the consequence.

For me, this step of the written consequence that brings in the administration is always a last resort. It is important to remember that you do not want to hand over your power or respect to another staff member. I have found that teachers who write referrals too often lose control of their classrooms. The students are no longer concerned about respecting them, because all of the discipline problems are outsourced.

You also want to be mindful that too many written consequences will cause this discipline strategy to lose its effectiveness. Students will likely begin to feel that you give "everyone" a referral for "everything." The risk is that students may no longer feel that they have done anything wrong because the severest consequence has become the norm. You have taken the sting out of it.

I write about two referrals a year, so my students are very afraid when they hear that word, because they know that it is not something they hear very often. Just be sure that all of your consequences have meaning and are purposeful. If you are creating written consequences out of frustration or helplessness, you will quickly find yourself having no control of your class.

Up to this point, I have offered a number of strategies about not letting things slide, but it is equally important to know when and how to let some stuff go. I find that I use the "Don't let it slide" method frequently in my classroom, because I do not want students to think that their misbehaviors go unnoticed; however, I rely heavily on the "Let some stuff go" method when it comes to how I issue consequences. Often the mere act of addressing the misbehavior—whether with discrete nonverbal cues, verbal corrections, or a brief conference—is enough to stop the misconduct, and there is no need for any further consequence or punishment. Ironically, by not letting the infraction slide (and using the least amount of intervention necessary), I am able to ultimately let it go.

Don't Give Power to Cursing

In your classroom, you may encounter students who curse, especially if you teach middle school or high school. Some teachers perceive cursing to be an extreme offense, but in my opinion, this attitude only gives the problem behavior more power than it deserves. Avoid this trap. Do not give your students the impression

"Remember to take the discipline approach that gets you back to learning as quickly as possible while building trust with your students."

that you are the cursing police; it will only encourage them to do it more and give them an easy way to disrupt your lessons and get under your skin.

Cursing does not have to be a written or referable offense. Assess each situation individually before making a decision about how to handle it. For example, when students curse in my classroom while talking to their friends, I simply remind them that cursing is not an appropriate form of communication while at school. Most students apologize and the class continues on with minimal disruption. However, if a student curses out of anger toward another person (including me), I usually address this behavior with a consequence. It may be necessary to remove the disruptive child from the room or refer him or her to an administrator. I do not make it my responsibility to control the way students talk outside the classroom. My concern is that they respect our learning environment within the building.

Take It Case by Case

Always bear in mind that discipline is not black and white. You should not run your classroom in absolutes. When unwanted behaviors occur, deal with them on a case-by-case basis. All children are not the same and should not be treated that way. My students understand that I run my classroom based on fairness not equity, by which I mean I choose my discipline approach based on the student's individual situation and needs—and those vary widely. Some students may need some extra guidance and redirection, whereas others may be repeat offenders who need you to hold them more accountable. Time and practice will help you develop a gauge for what kind of interventions your students need. I like to consider a child's behavioral history in my class before giving a consequence. I am often more willing to give students a chance if their behavior is uncharacteristic versus those whose behavior is always a problem. They have already used their grace period. Your concern is the way your students conduct themselves in your classroom, but keep in mind that students are bringing a lot of different needs into your learning environment, so dole out discipline with plenty of understanding and respect.

The Corn

"I'm sorry, Alisa. You can't participate. Those are the rules."

I slid my books off the table and slowly walked to the last seat at the farthest end of the room.

The other students were seated together chattering and giggling. Their conversations were inaudible, but I could tell that they were having a great time. As I sat slouched in my chair, forced to be an observer, I could feel a tear escape from my eye and run down my cheek. I quickly brushed it away and looked around to see if anyone noticed. But no one did. It was as if I were not there. It had only been 10 minutes since the lesson began, and I had already been forgotten. Even my best friend Emily did not look back to see if I was okay.

I didn't understand. I sat there blaming myself for forgetting to remind my mother about the corn. I blamed her for forgetting to make the corn. I cursed her single parent mind for always having too much to remember, for never having enough space for it all.

I was missing the finale to the class project. We had studied all month about South American cultures and were celebrating with a traditional feast. I had forgotten to bring in my food item, and my teacher would not allow me to participate. The torture continued when she made me stay in the classroom while the other students enjoyed the celebration. I was heartbroken. My 3rd grade mind could not conceive this form of cruel and unusual punishment. I wanted to run out of the room. I wanted to make up some excuse to leave.

As a child, I was sad and confused about my teacher's unwillingness to allow me to participate. As an adult and an educator, I find her behavior unnecessary and hurtful. Always remember that children are not responsible for their parents' actions. Rules are not always black and white. There are times when we must bend or change the rules in order to do what is best for our students. That teacher may have never thought about what she did to me that day ever again, but I carried that pain into adulthood and chose never to penalize my students for situations beyond their control. Remember that there is always a time when we have to "let some stuff go."

Start Again with a Clean Slate

Classroom management will go much more smoothly if you commit to starting each day with a clean slate. If you hold on to what students do and say from one day to the next, you will find yourself losing patience with your students easily. It becomes a vicious cycle: Your students act up, you hold onto your frustration about it, and then you begin waiting for your students to act up again—which they surely do. Your attitude goes from positive and trusting to negative and distrusting, and of course your students notice and, as a result, act out even more. The best thing to do to break this cycle is to remind yourself *constantly* to avoid taking any student misbehavior personally. It can be tough, but you can do it. Consciously work at letting go of the negative behaviors from the previous day. Remind students that while their negative choices sometimes end in consequences, it does not mean that you ever stop caring. Care and discipline are not antithetical. Caring teachers actually show that they care by establishing rules and procedures and then upholding them. It's how you let your students know that they can trust you and your word. But good discipline never holds grudges. Allowing students to see that you are willing to give them a second chance—and a third and a fourth and so on—will often help a student turn around. Most students will not want to let down a teacher who believes in them. This approach will help you maintain a positive relationship with even your most challenging students.

Opportunity for Reflection

Take a moment and think back to a recent conflict in your classroom. Reflect on your behavior during this disruption. Was there something you could have done differently? Was there anything you would change if you were in that situation again? How did your actions escalate or deescalate the conflict?

Sometimes as the adults in the room, we do not realize that our actions are also part of the problem. Don't be quick to believe that students are solely to blame for classroom management issues. It can often be us, the teachers, who need to readjust our attitudes and practices. It is important to hold ourselves accountable as well. Teachers and students both contribute to classroom dynamics.

Keep It in the Family

I grew up in a family where even as small children, we knew not to tell the family business to outsiders. Most elementary teachers learn fairly quickly which students have been taught this lesson and which have not. Now as an adult, I use the "keep it in the family" method when I am dealing with my students. There are very few things that I outsource to administration. A great way to build trust with your students is to not always "tell on them." When one of my students is doing something wrong, my first instinct is to handle it myself. As a middle school teacher, I also have teammates, so my second line of defense against problem behavior is to send the misbehaving student to a colleague's classroom. This way the problem is still "in the family." Only after a child's behavior cannot be corrected within the team do I ask for help from administration.

There are also a lot of things that I allow to slide instead of making a big issue about them. If a child is doing something that only affects his or her learning, then I usually address it in house. For example, a student's refusing to do an assignment is not a problem that merits a referral. If the student is sitting in silent defiance without disturbing anyone, then simply leave him or her alone. Later, try talking with the student about it, and be sure to follow up with an email to the parents.

Another example may be a child who talks routinely during independent assignments. Once again, this behavior is not a major offense. Have the student work in another teacher's classroom or send him or her to the hall to finish the assignment. Just be mindful of the option you choose. Some teachers' rooms may be noisier and more distracting than yours. Choose a colleague that has a calm classroom environment. The hallway can also pose a similar problem. If you know that your classroom is on a hallway with a lot of foot traffic, avoid sending students to the hall to work.

Students breaking small rules like eating in class, chewing gum, and using their cell phones are all things that can be handled in house. Middle school and high school students are old enough to understand when a teacher is giving them a break. They are often more receptive to your discipline if they believe that you are not always trying to report them to administration.

The goal is to maintain the learning environment. You don't want students to feel that they can get away with misbehaving, but you also do not want them to believe that you are against them. Once students believe that you are "out to get them," they will not be willing to do their best in your class. Student may comply for fear of getting in trouble, but the positive relationship is gone. And with enough students feeling this way, the positive learning environment will be gone as well.

Deal with the Ringleaders

My hope is that the majority of your students behave wonderfully, but the reality of education is that you will most certainly have students who seem to always have behavior problems and who encourage misbehavior in others. These students may even be extremely defiant or disrespectful. The first thing that you must do when a discipline problem like this arises is to assess the situation and the child individually. There have been times when I have had one or two students who were "ringleaders" of behavior problems and yet all the other students were still able to do well and follow directions.

Under this circumstance, I address those students individually. I speak with their parents. I have personal conferences with them about the expectations of the classroom. My goal is to keep these disruptive students from influencing other students to misbehave. It is also easier to regain control of the class when you only have a few discipline concerns in the room. You can remove those students and the disruption they cause by asking them to work in the hall or asking a colleague to take them when they are having a bad day. Use your resources and your allies (parents, other teachers, and administrators) to keep these disruptive students' influence to a minimum. (See "Strategy #3: Find Allies" for more tips.)

Cut Off Mob Mentality

Your classroom culture and your control over it can change significantly when the majority of your class presents behavior problems and only a few students are willing to cooperate. In this case, you have to do more to regain control. The first step is to find out which students have parental support. Contact the parents of all the students who have discipline concerns. Often there are some who have parents who will work with you to make sure that their child is not misbehaving.

The next step is whole class consequences. I often give whole class silent lunch or alter my lesson plans for class periods that I believe cannot handle an engaging activity. The point is to minimize the number of students with behavior problems. Most students want to do well and enjoy class. Once they see that their actions are keeping them from enjoying some of the luxuries afforded to their peers, you will see their actions change.

You can reduce the likelihood of having a completely disruptive class by setting your procedures up front as well as clearly and frequently communicating your expectations. Students usually become majority defiant when there is time and opportunity for misbehavior or ambiguity about what you expect from them. (See "Strategy #4: Create Effective Lesson Plans" for more information about how to manage expectations and establish procedures.)

Protect Your Safe Space

Be careful with defiant students who are violent or aggressive. Don't ever engage in an argument with them. Some defiant students try to create conflicts in order to get their teachers to argue in front of the class. Even if you are extremely upset, don't reciprocate this type of behavior and don't allow your students to see your anger or your fear. Focus instead on staying calm. Remember to pause and take a few deep breaths before responding to an angry, defiant student. It's okay to be silent for a few moments. Your goal is to deescalate the situation. If a student yells or becomes violent, you must protect your classroom as a safe space—it is one of your crucial roles as a teacher, and you are not responsible for it alone. Use your resources and remain calm.

If you can, quietly and assertively tell the defiant student to leave the classroom. If you feel the outburst is minor and the student will calm down with time alone, tell him or her to step to the hall and wait for you to come talk. Give plenty of time for the student to cool off, 5-10 minutes at least, but keep an eye out to make sure the student stays put. An outwardly angry student should never be allowed to wander the halls unattended.

If the student is past the point of calming down—if he or she is no longer defiant but openly aggressive, by which I mean threatening or attempting to harm you or anyone else—immediately call for an administrator or resource officer to escort the student away from your room for further intervention. Do not wait. *At no point should you put yourself or any of your other students at risk—use your resources, trust your gut, and call for help when you need it.* Always remember, your goal is to get the learning environment back to a safe space. Never try to restrain or placate an aggressive student. Once a student becomes violent, the best thing to do is get immediate help from the appropriate staff.

Hopefully, by implementing all of your classroom procedures, you will never have to deal with a situation like this. But if you do, be prepared. Know ahead of time how you will handle it and what steps you will take to regain control of your classroom so that you don't have to make those decisions in the moment, when emotions are extremely high. Also, bear in mind that combative students are often angry for reasons beyond your control. There are so many things influencing your students' lives, and you are just one of them. So if you encounter an angry student, do your best to defuse the situation before it escalates, but know that your first priority is always safety.

Welcome the Turnaround

Be careful not to prejudge students. It is very easy for teachers to just take the word of a colleague about a child's behavior or work ethic. This is a mistake. Try to avoid engaging in conversations about student behaviors from previous years. If you do hear things about your new students, remain positive and optimistic. I have found that oftentimes, after listening to other teachers, I do not have the same experiences. You are not aware of everything that took place in the previous teacher's classroom, so it is unfair to judge that a student will react in the same way in your classroom. If you are given information about a student, just take it as an opportunity to be alert.

Never count a child out before you meet him or her. Children are aware that teachers talk. I have had several students come up to me and ask what I have heard about them. They say things like, "My teachers told you I was bad, didn't they?" or "Did she tell you I got in trouble a lot last year?" This kind of questioning shows that these children care about the perceptions I have of them. I answer their concerns by saying that I don't know anything about them. I let them know that I look forward to learning more. I end this kind of conversation by reassuring my new students that whatever happened last year is in the past and that they have an opportunity for a clean slate with me.

While students who frequently act out offer the greatest challenges, they can also offer the sweetest rewards. When, as a teacher, you reach a "difficult" child, it is the truest sense of accomplishment. Try to look at these students and their behavior problems as an opportunity for you to grow as a teacher. Students who pose the hardest challenges tend to have strained home lives, below grade-level academic achievement, and trouble controlling their emotions. These children offer educators the most opportunities for growth and reflection. They require that we go beyond our normal, everyday planning and think outside the box to make real, genuine connections with them.

Always give these students an opportunity for turnaround. You may be the support they need to change in a positive direction. Remain calm and optimistic. Be encouraging even when it seems impossible. Never allow these children to feel that you have given up on them. A defiant child is often a defeated one. They are the children who feel that school has gotten too difficult. These are the children who act out because of frustration or feelings of inadequacy. Do not fuel those feelings. Encourage the opposite when you hear doubt. I am realistic. I do not tell students that they are doing great when they are not, but the goal is for them to show growth and progress. These are accomplishments you can celebrate with any student, regardless of their abilities or past behaviors. You can build them up and encourage them to achieve greater things.

Remember the Positive

Often as teachers we are so busy dealing with negative behaviors that we forget to address the positive ones. Whatever challenges you may be facing, make sure that you take time to recognize students who are doing well. It is important to reward students not only for academic accomplishments but also for behavioral achievements. Encouraging good character development is a huge part of effective classroom management.

Verbal praise is the easiest way to reward students—and it costs nothing! Fill your classroom with positive comments. Compliment students when they work hard. Offer praise when they answer a question correctly. Hand out written praise to infuse even more positive energy into your classroom. Encourage students to give positive feedback to each other whenever possible; it will help you build a sense of community and allow you to model positive ways for students to interact with one another.

"No, I Don't Have Any Candy!"—Some Thoughts on Rewarding with Sweets

Many teachers like to give candy and prizes in order to get students to follow directions. This tactic can prove to be problematic. If you are giving out candy to encourage students to cooperate with your instructions, you may begin to see that they are only willing to follow your directions if you offer a treat first. Some students watch the patterns of their teacher's discipline plan and look for ways to take advantage. I have heard several teachers talk about how they can no longer get their students to do anything without the promise of a treat. While it can be fun to reward students this way, I make it a rule to give out candy very sparingly.

My advice: Only give candy for major test results or whole class incentives. Do not make giving candy rewards a daily or weekly practice. It becomes less like a reward and more like a bribe for compliance. Also, be careful how you frame the reward. I do not tell my students ahead of time that there will be a treat or reward waiting for them. I want them to complete the assignment or follow my directions because it is the right thing to do. Only after the assignment is over do I surprise the students with a treat. This helps them to see that sometimes there are rewards for doing the right thing, but they are not expecting the reward. The goal is to teach students the correct way to behave in the classroom as well as in society. You do not want the focus to be centered on receiving a reward for what should be routine behavior.

Belonging

"What's going on over there?"

"Oh, nothing. Those students are just signing up for honors Language Arts."

"Well, why wasn't I invited? My grades are good, and I have been doing well all year."

"Very well then, go over and sign up, Alisa, but you probably won't like it. It's a lot of extra work."

[The Next School Year, About 3 Months In]

"Oookay...thank you, Jacob, for that very...interesting... interpretation. Alisa, you are up next."

I rose from my seat slowly and walked to the front of the classroom, my "Sinner in the Hands of an Angry God" mobile and speech in hand. I had spent all weekend rehearsing my speech and creating my visual. The mobile was simple, created with meticulously cut-out construction paper and string, polished up by the lamination my mother had done for me the day before. When I arrive at the board, I hung my mobile and began.

The class sat silently in awe—or maybe it was just quiet compliance—but for me it did not matter which. What mattered was what my teacher said when I finished and began to head back to my seat.

"Great job, Alisa. I can see that you belong here."

I'm sure that at some point I had been discussed—the little black girl who had dared to sign herself up for an honors class without a recommendation. My teacher probably does not remember this moment, but for me it was a turning point. It allowed me to see that I could do more than what people expected of me. I could challenge myself in advanced classes and succeed. I went from a shy kid in remedial Language Arts class to a confident teen who had proven that she "belonged" in honors Language Arts. The confidence I gained from this moment helped me to go on to earn three degrees and to share my knowledge and experience with you by writing this book.

As teachers, we do not know what fires we are starting, which dreams we are fueling or extinguishing. I learned from this experience to always lead with encouragement. Because of this teacher's encouragement, I was able to finish my high school career with confidence in honors classes. I remember the feeling of having that adult validation at school. That is the feeling I want to leave with my students.

"As teachers, we do not know what fires we are starting, which dreams we are fueling or extinguishing. Always lead with encouragement."

Strategy #3:

Find Allies

Teammates

Sitting in the vast cafeteria. Waiting for the most important news of the day. The new teams for next year. My heart races. A new chapter is about to begin…

"Hey, so I guess we are working together."

Smiles.

The year starts and so does our journey.

Eating breakfast. Grading papers. Eye rolls at meetings.

"Hey, are you okay?"

Tears.

Your boyfriend. My boyfriend.

My mother. Your mother.

Love.

"Hey, it's going to be okay."

Hugs.

Your father. My grandmother.

"Hey, you're going to get it."

Your house! My house!

"Hey, we did it!"

Cheers and laughter.

Your move. My move.

"Hey, we will always be teammates."

Always friends.

Teachers cannot make a difference by themselves. The best teachers have support from parents, administrators, other teachers, family, and friends. Teaching is a difficult job that becomes even more challenging without support. Make sure that you ask for help from others early. Get some allies. Use the beginning of the school year not only to make connections with your students, but also to build positive, trusting relationships with the other adults associated with your school. Having the support of others who are invested in your students will prove to be immensely beneficial to you later on in the school year.

Parents

No one will know and understand your students better than their parents. Getting them in your corner early on will go a long way toward your effective classroom management. Parents can reinforce your discipline strategies at home by reiterating school expectations and issuing their own consequences that support yours. Parent allies can also help make sure students are continuing to learn when they leave school. Try implementing the following strategies to begin making allies among your students' parents.

Make a Good First Impression

Parents can be your best allies or your worst enemies; therefore, it is important to get your students' parents on your side as early as possible during the school year. I start with registration day. Once you meet the parents for the first time, be sure to follow up with an email or phone call to let them know that you are excited about working with them to help their children succeed. I also like to send out as many positive emails as possible during the beginning of the school year. You want parents to feel good about their children being in your class.

Appearing professional in front of parents is another important way to gain their trust. Be sure to dress up a little more than usual when you know there will be parents in the building. While you want to be comfortable, you also want to be taken seriously. You are a professional, and it is vital that you present yourself as one. Your style of dress not only reflects your personality but also the amount of respect you have for yourself, your students, and your profession. Remember that when parents meet you for the first time, you should look your best.

Also, be mindful of your classroom's appearance. Just as you would clean up before having company at your home, you should do the same when inviting guests into your classroom. Your classroom is a representation of you. Remember that parents are taking note of all these things when they meet their child's teacher for the first time. Every parent wants to feel that his or her child is receiving the best education possible. When your classroom starts to become messy and chaotic, it's a good first sign that you're losing control of it. Stay on top of the clutter. Being organized will help you maintain an environment conducive to learning.

Most parents enjoy being informed of what is going on at school even if they do not always respond. I send out reminders before any major test or quiz. I also send reminders about important paperwork or class field trips. Parents seem to be more receptive and cooperative when they feel that you are willing to keep them informed. Allowing parents to see that they are a part of the process early on will help when you need their support later in the year.

Communicate Strategically

As a new teacher, you will have so many demands on your time and energy. Communicating with parents will be just one piece of that, but it will be a critical part of your job that you will not want to shortchange. Nonetheless, always remember that you do not have hours and hours to write emails and make phone calls. You must be strategic about how you communicate with parents not only to protect your valuable time and energy, but also to make sure that you are building strong relationships that could afford you some potential allies when you need them most.

Guidelines for Strategic Communication with Parents

1. **Contact parents about positive behaviors before negative behaviors arise.** Once the year is in full swing, you are going to have some students who misbehave, and you will have to start contacting parents about negative behaviors. It always helps if parents have heard from you already regarding something positive.

2. **Start and end every communication with something positive.** Sometimes it can be difficult to think of positive comments, but you will find that parents are more receptive to you when the entire communication—whether it's an email, a call, or a conference—is not negative. Reassure them that no matter what the situation, you are willing to work with them and their child and that you only have their child's best interest in mind.

3. **Stick to the facts and always be polite.** You never want your negative emotions to come through in an email, nor do you want to suffer through an angry call with a parent. If you are upset about an issue,

wait a few hours before contacting the misbehaving students' parents. Try to be as polite and concise as possible. I always end my emails with, "Thank you for your continued support." Although I may not be receiving support from every parent I email, it still allows them to see what I would like to have from them.

4. **Do not wait longer than 24 hours to contact a parent after an offense has occurred.** You want parents to know that you value their concerns. Waiting too long to respond with a call or an email can send the message that you do not care about the parents' perspective. Certainly wait until you can keep your cool if it is a high-stress situation, but do not let it go past a full day after the event.

5. **Opt for email over phone calls whenever possible.** Because you never know how long a phone call with a parent may take, protect your valuable time by sending brief and succinct emails to parents whenever you can. I often use phone calls as a last resort.

6. **Don't waste time writing lengthy e-mails.** If you feel that the email is going to take more than five sentences to explain the situation, then it is best to make a phone call or have a face-to-face conference to address the issue. Just remember to document everything.

7. **Document, document, document.** Emails are an easy and effective way to document your communication with parents, especially if you copy (cc) your administrators; however, you do not want to email about everything when a call or a conference may be more time-efficient. With these kinds of communication, you will want to be extra diligent with your note-taking and document the entire dialogue, including the date and time. Many schools have a form designated for this purpose as well.

8. **Use the school phone, not your personal phone.** Most parents are very nice and respectful, but you do not want your personal phone number to get into the hands of an angry parent who may misuse it.

9. **Allow for at least 15 minutes for phone calls.** You do not want parents to think that you are trying to rush the conversation with them. Be polite and listen attentively, but also be as brief as possible and always stick to the facts about any discipline problems.

10. **For serious discipline issues, communicate by phone first.** Emails often leave too much room for misinterpretation. If you feel that the infraction warrants a lengthier dialogue than a 15-minute phone call, use the initial call to set up an in-person conference with the student's parents.

11. **Set up conferences with parents before misbehavior escalates.** Trust your intuition. If you anticipate certain students are going to need more discipline, set up conferences with their parents at the first sign of trouble. Intervening early will often help prevent future misbehaviors and it will bring parents in as your allies from the start. Parents usually appreciate knowing what is going on before consequences become severe.

12. **Speak to parents, not to translators.** As a whole, schools are becoming very diverse. If you are in a conference speaking with a parent whose first language is not English, be sure to look at the parent when speaking. Do not speak directly to the translator. Remember that the parent is the person you're communicating with. Although he or she may not understand what you are saying, the respectful thing to do is to always address the parent.

Get 'em with the Grades

If you ever have trouble getting parents to show concern about their child's behavior in your class, you can almost always get their attention by bringing up grades. Keeping parents regularly informed of their children's progress is a highly effective way to keep an open line of communication going and to find parent allies. When my students have a missing assignment or receive a failing grade, I often let their parents know. It is a sad reality that many parents in fact do *not* know how things are going for their children in school. Keeping that communication open, honest, and frequent will be helpful to everyone. Emailing parents about upcoming tests or letting them know when a child is doing poorly will help parents feel that you are supporting their child's success.

Keeping parents in dialogue about grades may take some additional time and planning, but it will help you gain more allies than enemies. Because I always go this extra mile, I have found that when I call about a discipline problem, my students' parents are usually willing to lend their support. The goal is to show parents that you are doing everything you can to help their child succeed— that you are their ally as well.

Be Prepared: Parent Types

Though it may seem generalizing, being able to identify parent types can be incredibly useful. Recognizing the different kinds of parent personalities you will likely come into contact with can help you create the most effective alliances possible. Acknowledging parent types will help you make decisions about how parents can be most supportive of you, as well as allow you to set realistic expectations for your parents.

The Invisible Parent

This is the parent you will rarely, if ever, see. Invisible parents tend to miss meetings and events at school, and they rarely respond to emails or phone calls. Rather than not caring about their child's education, the invisible parent is typically just very busy. They are always at work and have very little time to invest in school activities or volunteering. These parents care about their children like any other parent. They too want their children to do well.

Once you realize that you have students whose parents fall into this category, do your best to support them as much as you can. These students often need the most support during the school day because their parents' main focus is paying bills and sustaining their families. Be careful to separate these children's actions from their parents' inaction. It is easy to become frustrated or irritated with the entire family when problems arise. Keep in mind that the children are not to blame for what their parents do. Make sure that your response to your students is based on their actions alone.

In addition, be sure to continue to communicate with the invisible parent. Although they may be unresponsive, your invisible parents are often reading your communication; they just don't have the time or energy to respond. If you feel that there is some important information that the parents must see, send it via certified mail, or put an email receipt on your electronic communication.

The Helicopter Parent

This is the parent who is almost too involved. Helicopter parents volunteer for every school event. They are in constant contact with each of their child's teachers. As soon as a grade is posted, you can count on an email from the helicopter parent for some reason or another. These parents ask their children about their days and then, based on their responses, follow up by contacting their teachers. These parents are extremely proactive to the point that sometimes you may not even have an answer to their questions yet.

Be sure to respond to these parents; they will not go away if you ignore them. Use their involved spirit to your advantage. Ask them to volunteer in the classroom. This kind of parent is wonderful for a room parent or a field trip chaperone. Helicopter parents like to be involved. Allow their involved spirit to help positively impact all the students in your room. Respond to their emails with an assurance that their children are doing well. This kind of parents tends to have very bright and responsible children, and yet the helicopter parents often need constant affirmation of their children's success. To make an ally of helicopter parents, it will help if you reach out to them before they reach out to you. Keep them informed. They too just want the very best for their children.

The Typical Parent

Most parents will be the typical parent. They will attend meetings and conferences as needed, but they won't be as proactive as the helicopter parents. They will respond to emails and work with you to solve problems whenever you ask for their help. Typical parents usually have children that are doing average to well in school. They do not have a lot of concerns and are often pleased with whatever decisions you make as their children's teacher.

Maintain regular communication with typical parents, but otherwise, don't worry too much about them. They are often great allies, so call on them when you need to. You should not have any problems with this type of parent.

The Plot Twist Parent

The "plot twist" parent is someone who starts your relationship being friendly and supportive but turns on you once you have something negative to report. When circumstances inevitably fall short of perfection, the plot twist parent will quickly go from ally to enemy. Plot twist parents often turn to administration when they feel you have unfairly targeted their children.

While it is important to have meticulous documentation for every parent communication, the plot twist parent is the reason you will need it. Make sure to keep a call log, save emails, and document conference details. All of these will help you to stick to the facts when a plot twist parent files a complaint.

However, plot twist parents can still become a limited ally. They often have insecurities about their children just like the helicopter parents.

Once you realize you have plot twist parents, having the documentation to back up your position can sometimes aid in keeping them on your side. They need reassurance that everything is okay and that their concerns are not being ignored. Try involving your administrator when communicating with a plot twist parent. Usually the presence of administration will help this parent feel more comfortable.

These parents, like all others, just want to feel that their concerns for their children have been heard. These parents often just need sound documentation for everything. I do not advise trying to build any true partnership with these parents. I would keep them informed on their child's progress, but I would not solicit their help with any volunteer opportunities. They can be dangerous. When they feel threatened, they often try to make life harder for the teacher. Once you have recognized this parent type, be sure to inform your administration about the communication. Copying them on an email or setting up a meeting should keep you from having more problems in the future.

Stop and Reflect

Below are two examples of a phone conversation I had with a parent during my first year of teaching. The first is my recollection of the conversation as it actually happened, and the second is how I wished I had handled it.

Push Pin—The Reality

Parent: "Hello?"

Me: "Hello? Yes, may I speak to Mrs. Smith?"

Parent: "This is Mrs. Smith."

Me: "Hi, Mrs. Smith. This is Ms. Swain from Howard Middle School. How are you today?"

Parent: "I'm fine."

Me: "Great! I am calling because I wanted to let you know that David got detention today. He had a push pin in his mouth, and I asked him to spit it out. He did, because I saw it fall into the trashcan; however, he is getting detention because when I looked over again, he had another push pin in his mouth."

Parent: "Well, where is he getting all these push pins? We don't have push pins at home."

Me: (Thinking to myself) Is this lady seriously asking me where her child got the push pins from? Why does that even matter? (To the parent) "Well, I am sure that he pulled it off of my bulletin board. He was sitting right next to it. Ma'am the point is that he is in the 7ᵗʰ grade and should know not to put push pins in his mouth. He could get hurt."

Parent: "Why does he need detention? If the push pins were not there, then he wouldn't have them."

Me: "Ma'am, he is old enough to know right from wrong and his actions deserve a consequence."

Parent: "Well I don't know what kind of teacher you are, but my child will not be serving this detention."

Me: "If I do not have your consent for the detention, then he will have to serve another consequence."

Parent: "You are a ******. And I am not ****** signing anything! I ought to—"

Me: (Interrupting) "Ma'am, this conversation is going nowhere. I am hanging up now. Goodbye." (I hang up.)

A few moments later, the parent called my administrator to say that I was unprofessional for hanging up on her. Needless to say, this conversation jumped the tracks and ended up going in a completely different direction than what I had expected. And at the time, I could not have told you why. In that moment as a first-year teacher, I was simply angry and frustrated at what I perceived to be this parent's complete lack of understanding. How could she not understand that her son could have been seriously hurt if he had swallowed one of those push pins?! And I was simply trying to reinforce the lesson by giving him detention! Plus, I was defensive that she somehow felt that it was my fault for having push pins on a bulletin board to begin with (such dangerous and reckless behavior, right?).

Conversations like this one will happen; it is inevitable, no matter how good a teacher you are. My advice is to let yourself have your feelings, the anger and disbelief and frustration, but then once you have cooled off, take a look back at what you think may have gone wrong and how you might have done things differently. You cannot control the parent's reaction or the outcome, but you can control yourself, and that can influence the outcome in your favor.

Now I can see that some of the things I said to this parent and my own attitude going into the conversation (it was 5:00 on a Friday and I just wanted to go home) certainly contributed to her defensiveness and anger toward me. For example, I didn't begin the conversation on a positive note. I just jumped right into the problem. Then when she expressed her concern to me ("Well, where is he getting all these push pins?"), I became frustrated that she would even ask such a question and that she did not immediately see my point and support me. When I responded with, "Ma'am, the point is that he is in the 7th grade and should know not to put push pins in his mouth," she likely perceived my response as an implication that her son was either dumber than most 7th graders or that he had not been taught at home to not do something so dangerous. Of course, these were not at all the messages I wanted to convey, but they may have been how she took my well-intentioned comments. I was frustrated with her, and because of my lack of experience, I didn't know how to get her into my corner, to be my ally.

Now, after seven years' distance, here's how I wish the conversation had gone...

Push Pin—The Remix

Parent: "Hello?"

Me: "Hello? Yes, may I speak to Mrs. Smith?"

Parent: "This is Mrs. Smith."

Me: "Hi, Mrs. Smith. This is Ms. Swain from Howard Middle School. How are you today?"

Parent: "I'm fine."

Me: "Great! David is fine, too, but we did have an incident today that I wanted to tell you about. At one point, I saw David with a push pin in his mouth. I told him to spit it out, and he did, because I saw it fall into the trashcan. But when I looked over at him again later, he had put another pin in his mouth.

Parent: (Interjecting) "Well, where is he getting all these push pins? We don't have push pins at home."

Me: "I think he must have pulled them off the bulletin board. After I found him with the second pin in his mouth, I told him to give me all of the pins he had and I gave him a detention, because I expect him to follow my directions and not put himself in danger like that. I thought you would want to know so that you can talk with him about it too. He is a very smart young man, and I enjoy having him in my class. I know he can make better choices than that."

Parent: "But why does he need detention? If the push pins were not there, then he wouldn't have them."

Me: "I understand your concern. But we use push pins in our bulletin boards because we trust our middle-schoolers not to put something like that in their mouths; they are old enough to understand how dangerous that is. I know David is capable of understanding that danger, too, and I want him to know his safety is important to me. I moved him to a seat away from the bulletin board, but I also believe that because he did it a second time, he needs a detention to reinforce this lesson, and to let him know that I expect him to follow my directions.

At this point in the "revised" conversation, I would hope that the parent would be less defensive than in the original version, but sometimes parents are going to be defensive no matter what we say, so let's pretend that she is still upset with my choice of giving her son a detention.

Parent: "Well, I don't know what kind of teacher you are, but my child will not be serving this detention."

Me: "Okay, Mrs. Smith, I understand. I will make a note that you have refused to give permission for the detention, though I believe that the consequence is very fair for the behavior. It would not go on David's permanent record, but it would reinforce the lesson that he has to be safe and follow my directions. However, since you're refusing the detention, I will determine another suitable consequence for David. I will let you know what it will be once I have decided."

Parent: "You are a ******. And I am not ****** agreeing to anything! I ought to—"

Me: (Interrupting) "Mrs. Smith, I understand you're upset, but I will not stay on the phone while you are cursing at me. If you would like to try talking again on Monday, please let me know. Goodbye." (I hang up.)

So what did I do differently in this revised version? First, I started by letting her know that her son was okay. Often when parents receive calls from their children's school, they immediately wonder if something is wrong. Put parents at ease right away by telling them that their child is fine (i.e., safe and not sick or hurt). Next, I told her about the incident and didn't lead off with the detention; instead, I explained the circumstances leading up to the consequence. When the parent interrupted with her concern ("Well, where is he getting all these push pins?"), I addressed it and made it clear that I was looking out for her son the entire time (i.e., I had him spit out the pin, I didn't punish him the first time, and when it became an issue, I had him move away from the board). I presented a tone that conveyed that I was on her side—and David's— and that my ultimate goal was his safety.

Nevertheless, despite our best efforts as caring teachers, some parents will remain combative. I left the outcome of this revised conversation the same as the first—the parent getting angrier and calling my administrator—because I wanted to show how I would handle that kind of blow-up now. In the second scenario, I calmly acknowledged her feelings but I refused to let her continue cursing at me. I do not regret hanging up on her, because no teacher should endure verbal abuse like that. I am confident my administrator would support me in this decision, and I hope yours would too. However, I believe that in most cases, the outcome of this revised conversation would have been more positive and I could potentially have made an ally. This parent just needed some reassurance that she and her son were not a target. She needed to understand that my concerns were for her son's well-being and that I wanted to tell her about the incident to get her help keeping him safe. Most parents just need reassurance that we are all playing for the same team.

What I hope you will see from these conversations is the value of reflection. As educators, we always want to improve, to get better at our profession. That requires a lot of thinking about how we do what we do, and why we do what we do. My first year of teaching was a giant learning curve for me. There was so much about the profession that I did not know nor understand. After getting a few more years under my belt and having more experiences with parents, I now have much more confidence in my ability to keep parents as my allies.

Teachers

In addition to parent allies, you should make teacher friends—really good teacher friends. Because just as no one will understand your students better than their parents, no one will understand your life as a teacher, with all its joys and struggles, better than other teachers. Your family and friends will try—and they, too, are critical for your success—but there is nothing like the lived experience of being in the classroom day in and day out. You will need and want people in your life who have that experience and understand exactly what you are going through and can offer actionable support. I learned early on that life is much easier and much more fulfilling with a good set of friends who are a part of the profession. To find your teacher friends, start with your teammates and other teachers who work in your department. These colleagues are great because they know your students and/or your subject matter and can offer you valuable tips and suggestions about lessons, as well as help with classroom management.

Make a Variety of Teacher Friends

There are a number of different kinds of teacher friends you can make, each with different advantages and benefits that support your teaching career. The following are what I consider the most helpful types.

The Discipline Buddy

Your discipline buddy should be a friend or neighbor close to your classroom who is a no-nonsense teacher. Ask yourself, "Which teacher on the hall are my students most afraid of?" Then become discipline buddies with that person. When your students are being disruptive in your classroom and time out in the hallway just isn't enough, send them on over to your discipline buddy. Just be very careful in choosing this teacher. Never send your students to a teacher who is well liked or a teacher who struggles with classroom management. If the teacher already struggles with classroom discipline, it is very likely that your student will not be required to follow directions while in that classroom. The purpose of sending your disruptive students to your discipline buddy is to remove them from your classroom while also putting them in an environment where they are uncomfortable and would rather be in your class.

The Planning Partner

You want to spend your first couple of months working on your classroom management and lesson planning skills. Which teacher seems to have strong lesson plans and lots of resources? Get to know that teacher. Try to learn from him or her. Which teacher has a handle on classroom management? Ask that teacher questions. Learn what it takes to run a chaos-free classroom. Once you have had a few months of teaching, you will begin to notice which teachers are willing to be supportive and helpful. Those teachers are the ones that you want to be your "planning partners." It helps to have other teachers to share ideas with; however, be careful not to use your planning partners as a crutch. It is important to learn to plan and implement for yourself as well. The partnership should serve as a mentoring opportunity. More experienced teachers do not like to feel as though they are doing your job for you. Make sure that you are trying to contribute to the partnership as well. This will help you to keep this alliance longer. Many teachers do not mind helping new teachers, but they do not want to feel as though they are being used.

More Often Than Not, DIY—Do It Yourself!

Avoid just copying another teacher's lesson plans. Although this may seem like an easy way to handle planning as a new teacher, you will find very little value in it long-term. Also, I have found that it is difficult to properly implement lesson plans that I did not help create. Just embrace the process of being a new teacher. It will take you longer to plan, and you may struggle with classroom management at first. But it will be worth the struggle when you have what you need to be successful in the years that follow.

The Close Friend

It takes time to make close teacher friends. You do not want to make the mistake of befriending the wrong people who will only make your job more difficult, so be very careful not to make close friends too quickly. Ease into it. Get to know people. Built trust over time, just as you would with your students.

Because I have been in the profession for several years now, many of my close teacher friends do not work at my school anymore. These are the folks whom I have known for a long time, and while we haven't always stayed at the same school, their support remains invaluable. If you decide to socialize outside of work with other teachers, be careful not to speak negatively about your school.

Many teachers have found that this practice does not end well.

The benefit of the close teacher friend is having someone who understands very well what you are going through and who knows you well. Often people who are not teachers do not understand what teaching is really like. They may be sympathetic to your situation, but they do not really understand what life is like for an educator. Having close teacher friends can be a great support system. Identify teachers who you feel you can trust.

Administrators

Administrators are always important people to have on your side. You will at some point need their support in order to have an effective discipline plan. You often hear that administrators set the tone for the entire school and, ideally, that tone should mirror your own positive classroom culture. But even if you find yourself in a school-wide environment that is less than ideal, it will still be extremely helpful to be on good, respectful terms with your administration. In addition to helping you get the classroom materials you need, they can stick up for you if ever a conflict arises with a parent as well as help you deal with major discipline concerns in your classroom. But remember, the role of the administrator should be to serve as a support system for you, not your go-to source for discipline. Do not expect administrators to handle the majority of your discipline problems—that's your job!

Be the Bad Cop

I see it so often: New teachers want to be the "good cop" when it comes to disciplining their students and expect the administrator to be the "bad cop." They want to be well liked by their students, always understanding and sympathetic, while letting the administration dole out the heavy discipline. They think that they should be able to outsource their discipline problems and just deal with the wonderful children who want to learn.

The problem with this misguided strategy is that when you outsource your discipline problems—when you shy away from being the "bad cop"—you also relinquish your power. Once students realize that you do not have the courage and confidence to take charge of your classroom, they will begin to take charge of it for you. You do not want the students to feel that you are afraid to do your job. Because the truth is, you can be respected by your students, even liked by them, and still be strict with your classroom management; in fact, those teachers who are not afraid to be the leaders of their classrooms are often the *most* liked and respected by their students.

"When you outsource your discipline problems—when you shy away from being the 'bad cop'—you also relinquish your power."

Opportunity for Reflection

Think back to when you were a student. Can you recall a teacher who was very strict but whom you really liked and respected? How did he or she interact with students and run the classroom?

Don't Be the "Crying Wolf" Teacher

Not only does going to the administration with all of your problems show the children that you are not in control, but it also makes it more difficult for you to get support from your administrators. You become that teacher who is always complaining about students, never confident in your own abilities or willing to do the heavy-lifting of classroom discipline. Administrators have a lot on their plates, and they do not have the time or the resources to put out all the fires that will inevitably come up in your class.

You don't want to be the "crying wolf" teacher. In my mind, crying wolf teachers are the ones who always take their problems to the administration. They write a referral every week out of frustration and desperation. They press the panic button so much that administrators don't even respond to them anymore, because their concerns are no longer seen as valid. It has never been overtly said, but I have seen this happen many times with teachers who never got a handle on their classroom management. Even when there was a situation that needed administrative intervention, it did not get the attention it deserved because the administrators had become desensitized to the crying wolf teachers' problems.

The goal is to handle as much as you can without your administrator's help. Throughout this book, I offer tips and strategies about how to manage your classroom effectively. Use them to help you take control. You can do it! Remember to always keep your administrator informed, but not bothered. For example, when I am dealing with a difficult parent, I always send a copy of my correspondences to my administrator. I am not asking her to intervene, but I am making her aware of the situation. This way if there is ever a need to involve the administrator, it will not be her first time hearing about it. Administrators tend to respond better when they are a) kept informed and b) only directly involved as a last resort.

Get Them in Your Corner: Administrator Types

There are also different types of administrators to take into consideration. These are the ones I have encountered thus far.

The Cool Guy/Gal

The "cool" administrators are liked by all. Students love and respect them because they are fun and engaging, but students do not see them as disciplinarians. The cool administrator is often a very personable individual, someone who all students and teachers feel comfortable around. These administrators are very approachable, which yields both positive and negative results for them. The positive side is that they are people who teachers and students feel comfortable speaking with about problems and concerns; however, these administrators also frequently lose some respect. Students do not see them as disciplinarians, just as teachers do not see them as respected authority figures. Teachers and students tend to bend or break the rules when a cool administrator is in charge, because neither party is concerned about a consequence. Although cool administrators do sometimes give consequences for negative behaviors, it is often too lenient. Teachers and students alike don't mind taking the risk of being discovered. The cool administrators are often seen as weak and taken advantage of in that way.

In the event that you encounter this kind of administrator, it is very important that you have your own discipline plan and procedures in place. This type of leader is great for creating a mentor for your students but will offer very little in terms of help with discipline concerns. Try calling this kind of administrator in early in the process of dealing with a difficult student or parent. Because the cool administrator is such a people person, he or she will probably help smooth out the situation with parents and would also be a great resource for mentoring the students. Allow the cool administrator to be the "good cop." He works best in this role. You become the "bad cop" in the situation and set consequences and boundaries for your students. Instead of relying on this administrator, lean more on your colleagues and friends for support and suggestions in discipline matters.

The Tyrant

The tyrant administrator is only in it for him- or herself. Tyrants may be principals or vice principals for now, but it is obvious that they have other aspirations. These administrators only want things done their way. There is very little room for teacher choice and doing what works best for your students' needs. They are usually not open to suggestions or feedback, as they are concerned only with what the district numbers represent. The tyrant administrator operates on a personal plan versus a plan to see everyone succeed.

Because things that make them look good impress tyrants, you can usually make an ally of this type of administrator by just simply doing your best. Make sure that your students are on task and doing well during testing. Try getting involved in other programs around the school building.

Volunteer for some committees or an afterschool event. Once the tyrant sees that your efforts are leading to promoting the school in a positive light, you will have an ally. The point is to get the tyrant on your side so that you are free to focus on your students without worry of attack. The tyrant typically goes after teachers that he or she believes are not making the school better. This does not mean that those teachers are not actually doing great things; it just means that whatever they are doing is not obvious to the tyrant.

When working with a tyrant administrator, you will again need to adapt a discipline plan that works for you. However, you must be very careful to document all of the consequences and communications that you have made. This form of leader will not support you if a problem arises. Be sure to have documentation to prove that whatever you have done is legal and ethical. Take meticulous notes in meetings and quote the school expectations when questioned about your classroom practices.

The Supporter

This administrator is always there for you. Supporters are willing to do whatever is needed to help your students (and thereby you) succeed. This type of administrator is a great one to keep on your side. They will help you get the resources you need to create a wonderful learning environment. Supporters are usually very approachable. They will listen to your concerns and help you find anything you need to make your teaching/learning experience better. Supporters have usually been at the same school for several years because they are dedicated to the community and to the students. Supporters can also be great disciplinarians. Students tend to have a healthy fear of being called to their office. Supporters do not like it when students disrupt learning, so the punishments are often harsh but fair.

When dealing with disciplinary problems, be sure to explain how the student is disrupting the learning environment. The supporter's main concern is student success. If you phrase all of your discipline concerns in terms of student achievement, you will most likely get this administrator to support your decisions. Supporters would also become a fast ally if you become more involved in your school. They like to see teachers engaging with students during non-academic settings. Try going to a basketball game or volunteering to sponsor a club. Not only will your students appreciate your efforts but also your administrator. That way if a discipline situation does occur, the administration will be willing to help because they see that you care about your students as a whole and that is what matters to them.

Keep in mind that no matter what kind of administrator you are working with, it is your responsibility to handle your classroom environment. I have run my classroom the same way regardless of the leadership in the administrator's office. Make sure that you are perfecting your classroom management plan. Many teachers get caught up in what the administrator is or is not doing. Do not allow yourself to be concerned with this. If you have a sound plan, your classroom will be unchanged by the hands of leadership.

Family

Don't forget about your family. As a new teacher, your family members will be your first allies. They are the people you already know and trust. Don't be afraid to call on them for some resources and help. My mother is a retired educator, so I have the wonderful advantage of all her experience at my disposal. I was able to call her for tips and suggestions during my first year. She even went shopping with me to get materials for my first classroom. I still remember strolling through Target looking for items. She told me that I needed a small file box for my desk. I was hesitant because I did not want to get too much. She assured me that it would not go to waste. And it turns out that she was right. Every year that box is full of paperwork and documents that I am required to keep up with. At the time, I had no idea the massive amounts of paperwork that teachers have to deal with!

I guess her advice and counsel was her way of paying me back for the countless hours that I spent stapling papers, putting up bulletin boards, and rearranging desks—the life of a teacher's kid. It has come full circle for us. But the point is that when you need some assistance, sometimes the best help is right there in your household. Think of ways that your spouse and children can help alleviate some of your work stressors. What tasks can you ask them to assist you with? What gifts and talents do your family members have that would help make your job easier?

"Remember that your family is the constant in this journey."

Family members can also be great shoulders to lean on when you are feeling stressed at work and need someone to just listen. Try to avoid voicing all of your work concerns and stressors with coworkers. Leave those very real thoughts and feelings for your family members who understand your heart and will help you refocus on your reason for joining the profession. Remember that your family is the one constant in this journey. No matter which school you are in or which grade you teach, you will always be a part of the same family.

Students

Yes, students! Believe it or not, students are your allies, too. In fact, the most important alliance you make will likely be between you and your students. When students believe that you truly care about them, you will be able to manage their behaviors better, because they will trust you and want to make you proud. Throughout the school year, my students learn over and over again that I am not out to get them, that I will do my best to be on their side. Now, do I mess up and forget to honor these alliances sometimes? Of course. I make mistakes, and you will, too—you'll be heavy-handed, you'll get tired and quick-tempered, you'll lose your cool. But how you handle those moments will determine your success in forging those solid alliances with your students. Own up to your mistakes, apologize if it is warranted, and then move on. Get back to the business of learning and show your students what good character really looks like.

The Apologies

Class was getting started again after a twenty-minute lunch break, so I knew that the attention rate was going to be low. Some students were tired from the long day and others had shut off because it was 4ᵗʰ period and they no longer cared. But I forged on.

I began to explain the assignment when Brian barged in. I had been having an increase in tardies lately and was just so tired of these children thinking that they could come to class whenever they felt like it. I decided that I was not even going to ask Brian where he had been. When I had asked Amy yesterday, she replied, "I got lost." Yeah, right. She got lost. It was only the 100ᵗʰ day of school. So I just issued Brian a consequence. Short and sweet.

"Brian, you have silent lunch."

"What for? I was with Dr. Amous! You didn't even give me a chance to tell you!"

I had given him chances to explain before and it had been nothing but attitude…although, he had a point. Dr. Amous was Brian's mentor, an important relationship for him, and Dr. Amous did often keep Brian late. I decided to take away the silent lunch, but I would wait to tell him at the end of class. I didn't want to disturb my lesson any further, but I couldn't help making one more remark.

"Have a seat. You are late, and you are interrupting my class."

"Hey, man! That isn't fair," *another student, Jay, joined in.*

Brian stayed standing and continued his protests: "But this is so unfair! Why do I have silent lunch? You didn't even listen to me. I didn't do anything wrong!"

At this point it felt like a free-for-all when yet another student decided to weigh in.

"Yeah, but you are always doing something," *Matthew accused Brian.*

"Shut the fuck up, Matthew!" *Brian shouted back.* "No one was talking to you!"

True, I thought to myself, but he can't say that.

"Okay, Brian, now you have to leave the room," *I said in my calmest teacher voice.* "You can't just curse like that. Go next door to Ms. History."

After I refocused the class from this midday soap, I quickly finished my instructions and got the students started on the activity. As I passed the door that joined my room to Ms. History's, something told me to check on Brian. Sure enough, he was not there. I quickly alerted an administrator that I had a student missing and she assured me she would take care of it.

At the end of class, after the other students had gone to their elective, I was sitting at my desk grading papers when there was a knock at the door. It was Brian and Mr. Davis, the ISS teacher. I greeted them both. Brian began to apologize for his behavior. While he was apologizing, I started thinking about my own part in the conflict. Did I really have to give him another consequence, especially in front of the class like that? Technically, he was with his mentor, and it probably wasn't his fault he was late. He can't control when Dr. Amous lets him go. And I had been really frustrated because of all the tardies from everyone lately; maybe I took it out on Brian. And I was impressed that he chose to go to ISS to cool down instead of running off. When Brian finished talking, I accepted his apology and I apologized to him as well.

Strategy #4:

Create Effective Lesson Plans

The Overhead Projector

"I can't see!" shouted Sam, a freckle-faced boy seated on the second row, squinting as he repositioned his glasses.

"His head is in the way," exclaimed Kimberly as she stretched to the right of her chair, trying to look around the boy in front of her.

"The screen is too small!" protested Valencia, a tall girl from the front row.

"Why are we using this?" asked Max while sharpening his pencil at the sharpener by the door.

It was obvious at this point that I was quickly losing the class. When I planned to use the overhead projector for the grammar lesson that day, it seemed like a great idea. I could write directly on the slides to demonstrate for my students how to correct grammar mistakes in the sentences I had prepared. It all made perfect sense that morning before school as I planned my lesson and gathered my materials. But now it was clear my plan had failed.

"Do we have a volunteer who would like to correct the next sentence?" I inquired, hoping to get the focus back on the lesson.

One very shy young lady from the back of the classroom raised her hand.

"Ah yes, Sarah, come on up."

Sarah made her way to the projector, and I handed her the marker. As she began writing, the students continued with their complaints. It was evident that this lesson was a sinking

> *ship with no possibility of being saved. I wanted to abort the mission, but I had no backup plan.*
>
> *Upon reflection, it was clear why my plan hadn't worked. The overhead was outdated. It no longer had the ability to be used as a proper learning tool. The students had become accustomed to the larger, more modern forms of projection in the classroom. Their fixation on the overhead as a foreign and antiquated piece of equipment made it impossible for them to focus on the grammar lesson. This would be the overhead's final lesson—and my last time without a backup plan!*

Lesson planning is a very important part of effective classroom management. Many teachers lose their students' attention when they are not adequately prepared for the lesson, and once students are no longer on task, you have lost control of your classroom. So start each week with a plan for what you are going to do each day. Of course, as teachers, we know that things are always subject to change, but having a plan (and a backup plan!) will cut down on your stress for the week and make classroom management easier.

If you are a new teacher, don't be afraid to ask for help. Consult other teachers about which lessons have worked best for them in the past. Sometimes we have great ideas in theory but in practice they do not work with actual students. Ask a fellow teacher to review your lesson plans or explain to them your lesson idea. Collaborating with other teachers can be a great asset for a first-year teacher or a teacher changing grade levels or content areas. (See "The Planning Partner" in Chapter 2.)

Know Your Learners

A crucial part of the lesson planning process is to know your learners. Who are you planning your lessons for? Do they have any special needs or concerns that must be addressed? Do all of the learners in the classroom require the same lesson and activities, or do you need to plan for more variety and modifications? It is important to consider these questions before you begin to create your lesson plans, because meeting the needs of *all* of your learners—not just some or most—will cut down on student disruptions.

Do some research on each of your students and their academic needs before the school year begins so that you will have a general idea of how to structure your lessons. Then observe your students closely throughout the year and make adjustments as necessary. Bear in mind that students will normally not advocate for themselves. When a lesson is too difficult or they do not understand, they will sit and talk or distract others rather than ask for help. When a lesson is too easy, your students may finish quickly and choose to take a nap or talk to other students while they wait for something else to do. Most students will not articulate their educational needs. It is your job to be aware of them and then plan accordingly.

Strategies for Common Learner Types

Every student will learn at his or her own pace, but understanding the broad types of learners that may appear in your classroom can help you find a starting point to begin meeting your students' unique needs. Meeting students "where they are at" (as opposed to where you—or perhaps more accurately, the state—would like them to be) can help ensure a classroom environment that is affirming of all learner types.

> "Most students will not articulate their educational needs. It is your job to be aware of them and then plan accordingly."

General Education Learners

General education learners are those students who are usually on or near grade level. These students have a wide range of abilities. They are usually the students who can handle the standards as given. Even within the general education population, there are some vast differences. Determine what the point is for your lesson, what you are trying to teach. If certain elements can be changed to help students succeed, make the necessary adjustments.

Advanced-Level Learners

Advanced or high-level learners enjoy working independently. High-level students typically dislike group projects because their advanced performance and leadership qualities make them susceptible to doing the majority of the work. If you choose to do group work with advanced students, they prefer to be placed with other high-level learners. Give them plenty of choice. Try allowing these students to have self-guided or self-directed assignments. Give them the parameters and allow their minds to explore. Allow them to make decisions about what they learn and how in-depth they want to go. They like having ownership of their learning process. Often advanced-level learners have been tested and shown to be gifted. As a result, these students require that teachers create more rigorous lessons in order to challenge their bright minds.

Gifted and high-level students are often avid readers. Because they enjoy reading, these students are often fast learners. It is important to pump up the rigor when teaching gifted learners. They also have very curious minds, so be prepared for lots of in-depth questions and abstract thinking.

Low-Level Learners

Classes with a majority of low-level learners will need lots of partner work and demonstrations in order to complete assignments. Low-level learners require support that helps guide them toward the answers. For example, when reading a story in class, I like to listen to an audio version instead of having students read it aloud. Low-level learners are often poor readers. They will be too concerned with the decoding of words and sentence fluency to focus on the meaning of the text. For this reason, I play the audio, and stop periodically to check for understanding. This takes away the students' need to stress about reading out loud and allows them to focus on the ideas in the story.

Low-level learners typically do not do homework for a variety of reasons. I have found that using as much class time as possible to review concepts works best. I run my classroom as if the material will not be reviewed again until the students return the following day. I always give these students additional opportunities to study and practice during class. I also try to pair them with students who may be able to help them while I am assisting other students. You don't want the low-level learners to feel defeated. Be sure to celebrate even small areas of growth.

Special Education Learners

A special education student is one who has an identified educational or physical disability. This disability has been diagnosed and the child has been given an IEP (Individual Education Plan). An IEP is a legal document that tells teachers what accommodations a student is allowed to have in the classroom in order to help him or her be successful. Be sure to follow everything in this document. It is a legal document, so teachers who do not follow it can open themselves up to legal consequences. Special education students require additional support. They usually require more time and attention in order to understand tasks and assignments. When working with a special education student in the general education classroom, you will also have a special education teacher working with you. This is extremely helpful. Talk to the special education teacher about what accommodations you should make to support your students. They are the experts on the laws, and they are responsible for knowing some strategies for helping these students.

If you are not familiar with a kind of learner that has been placed in your class, be sure to consult with an administrator or another faculty member for support. You want to make sure that you are preparing your lessons to meet the demographic of students you actually have. Rarely, if ever, will you have just one kind of learner in your room at a time; it will inevitably be a variety. Classrooms are composed of many different students all bringing their individual needs and concerns. Be sure to research each of your learners. Knowing the kinds of students that you have in your room will help you to plan more meaningful lessons. Lessons that cater to your learners will aid you in combating those behavior problems that come along with academic concerns.

Go Ahead and Generalize (a Little) about Gender

While we as teachers want to avoid the pitfalls of over-generalizing about our students, I want to encourage you to go ahead and generalize a little bit about gender and how it often plays out in classroom management. Whatever the reason—nurture or nature, biology or socialization—boys and girls tend to influence class dynamics in different and predictable ways. Being aware of this reality and adjusting your lessons and plans accordingly will help your teaching and classroom discipline become even more effective.

In my years in the classroom (both as a teacher and as a student), I have found some of the stereotypes to be true: Boys are often more physically active in class than girls. By this I mean they fidget a lot, look for reasons to get out of their seats, roughhouse with their friends—any number of things that involve them moving around a lot. For this reason, it is always good to have plenty of opportunities for movement and group work when you are dealing with a class of more boys than girls. Girls, on the other hand, tend to have fewer problems staying seated for an entire class period, but they are often extremely social. They want to talk with their friends, to talk more in general, so when you have a class with more girls than boys, give lots of opportunities to share or talk about their assignments. Paying attention to gender dynamics in your classroom will help you refrain from creating unrealistic expectations for your class.

Manage Expectations

When it comes to effective classroom management, it helps to prepare your students before you begin teaching. Let them know what's coming up and what you expect from them. Because when students have a clear expectation of what they will be doing, it is easier for them to follow through. It also helps to tell them when they will be able to talk or move again when you are giving instructions. It encourages them to stay focused, because they will know that a break or change in activity will occur soon. For example, if I want my students to pay close attention to my lesson, I explain to them that I am going to teach for a little while and afterward they will use the information I share with them to work in their groups. This clear and upfront communication helps students see that their quiet, focused attention is needed for a short time. They can then prepare themselves to focus. It reduces their temptation to talk during the lesson because they know that they will be given an opportunity to talk with their classmates again in a few minutes.

Pack the Class

If you are having trouble with students misbehaving during class, it is important to make sure that they do not have any down time. Pack the class full! Plan lessons that keep your students constantly working. Plan for more than what they could possibly complete in one class period. Often when students have lots of down time they get in more trouble. If students are concerned about being able to finish their work, there will be little time to goof off. I also like to plan ahead and have an assignment for students who finish early; it keeps the early finishers from distracting others.

Another way to pack the class is to have structured, timed activities. Make sure that students have a different activity every 10-15 minutes. Children have a very short attention span, so changing their activities frequently will help you keep more of your students engaged. Also, be mindful of the level of difficulty of the assignment. If students feel that the work is too easy or too difficult, they may not stay fully engaged. The skill of knowing which lessons to choose is one that develops over time. It is very important for new teachers to identify a friend or mentor who can help you make good decisions about appropriate lessons.

Bathroom Mayhem

After enjoying our twenty-minute lunch break filled with hustling through the halls, hasty restroom breaks, waiting in tedious lines, and only eight minutes of actual eating, my students and I were heading back to our classroom. As they filed in and found their seats, another teacher came up, clearly distressed.

"Ms. Swain, I need to see Alejandro!" demanded Mrs. Birdsong as she rushed through the door.

"Sure, what's going on?" I replied, startled by her abrupt entry.

"The boy's restroom is completely trashed," said Mrs. Birdsong. "There are wet paper towels and tissue all over the floor and ceiling, and five boys came out completely soaked! I am taking statements from each of the boys who were in the restroom at the time."

"But I didn't do anything!" protested Alejandro. "I just went to the bathroom and left!"

By this time all of the other students had completely abandoned their assignments for fear of missing the live entertainment that was taking place at the front of the room. Their heads moved back and forth from one speaker to the next like a professional tennis match, each of them intent on seeing how this was going to end.

"Alejandro, did you go to the restroom after lunch?" I inquired calmly.

"Yes, but I had nothing to do with that!" he cried.

"I'm not saying that you did. But we have classroom procedures for a reason," I gently reminded him. "Mrs. Birdsong's class goes after lunch. If you had gone before like we always do, you would not be involved in this. Go with Mrs. Birdsong now and write your statement."

"Man, this is so unfair," Alejandro bellowed as he exited the classroom with Mrs. Birdsong at his heels.

"I'm sorry, but there are procedures in place for a reason."

Focus More on Procedures, Less on Rules

Many people have the misconception that effective classroom management starts with enforcing rules, but good discipline actually starts with establishing and repeatedly practicing good procedures. These terms "rules" and "procedures" may seem interchangeable, but they are not the same. Procedures are the habits and routines you teach your students to follow every day to minimize disruptions and maximize learning time in the classroom. Rules, on the other hand, are the laws of your classroom that, if broken, are usually followed up with a consequence.

Procedures create structure and order in your classroom on a day-to-day basis. They help students clearly understand your expectations for them and for their behavior. For example, one of my procedures is that I always have my students place their bookbags under their desks or chairs as soon as they enter class. Because my classroom is not very large and space is always an issue, this procedure allows me to move around the room freely while I teach and saves me from having to repeatedly address the problem of clutter.

Another one of my procedures is having students read independently for 10 minutes at the beginning of every class. (You could also have them write in their agendas or complete a warm-up during this time.) This first procedure of the day helps me to start each class with a calm, structured activity, and it allows me to greet each of my students at the door and check attendance.

Without my having to remind them, my students know that after they enter my classroom and put their bookbags under their desks, their next step is to have a seat and take out their books to read quietly to themselves. They know that this is uninterrupted reading time. I do not allow restroom breaks or trips to the clinic during the first 10 minutes of class, and they know not to ask me for these privileges. Once the 10 minutes are up, the timer sounds and students put their books away, ready to listen to my instructions for the day. They know the expectation, and they are prepared to follow it daily.

Students need to be aware of the classroom expectations up front, from the very first day of class. Setting and practicing classroom procedures from day one will help reduce the need for heavy-handed rules and redirection in the future. If students forget to follow a procedure, a punitive consequence is rarely necessary; simply remind them of the procedure and have them practice it until it becomes routine. Good procedures go a long way toward helping minimize your discipline intervention. (See "Don't Let It Slide/Let Some Stuff Go" in Chapter 2 for more information.)

Enforcing rules, however, becomes necessary when procedures are not in place to begin with. When students lack structure, when they either are unsure of what to do or have no productive task to keep them focused, they are more likely to act out and break your classroom rules. Unlike a forgotten procedure that usually only requires a reminder or more practice, broken rules are often best reinforced with consequences. For example, one of your rules may be, "Treat everyone with respect." If a student breaks this rule, you will likely need to intervene with a consequence to help reinforce this important lesson, because there is no "procedure"—no routine or habit—to remind him or her of. Also, because it is more serious than something like leaving a bookbag on the floor, I recommend addressing this negative behavior more directly. A good general practice is to have only a few broad rules but many specific procedures.

Prevention vs. Cure

Think of the distinction between procedures and rules in terms of health—the health of your classroom:

Procedures are your prevention strategies for achieving and maintaining a healthy classroom environment. It's like the exercise, nutritious eating, and good sleep habits that keep your classroom from getting "sick" with misbehavior and disruptions.

Rules are the cure for these ailments when they occur. When good procedures aren't in place, when you haven't been doing the good prevention strategies and your students start acting out, enforcing rules is the "medicine" you need to treat and eliminate these problems.

For effective classroom management, you want to make sure you have more procedures than rules, and that you put the majority of your time and energy into clearly communicating and practicing those procedures so that enforcing rules becomes less and less necessary.

Some other examples of procedures:

- Sharpen your pencil only during non-instructional times.
- Place your writer's notebook in the basket at the end of class. It must always stay in the classroom.
- You may leave the classroom only when you have permission and no one else is out of class at the same time.
- You may use the materials on the table; they are for all to share.
- Ask before using materials on the teacher's desk.
- You may go to your locker at the beginning and end of class, but only by permission during the class period.

Finally, procedures foster greater responsibility in your students. All ages of school children are different, but they all have some level of independence. Create procedures that help students know what to do so that they do not need to ask you for everything. When you put some of the responsibility back on them, you will be able to focus on delivering the lesson or helping students who are struggling with the content. Decide which procedures will work best in your classroom. What can students handle without your assistance? Which freedoms and responsibilities would you like your students to have? What materials will they need? What should they do or write down first? Your goal is to set procedures that will allow for the most effective use of class time for all involved.

Add Some Effective Feng Shui

Like feng shui (the Chinese philosophy of spatial arrangement), how you arrange your physical space in the classroom can have a big impact on the success of your lessons and overall classroom management. It may not be intuitive, but taking some extra time to think about not only the content of your lesson, but also the space in which you deliver it will save you a lot of stress later. While you are planning, consider various classroom configurations and where you would like your students to direct their attention. For example, when I want my students to collaborate, I always rearrange the desks into groups. Grouping the desks encourages conversation because students are facing one another. On the contrary, if I want to discourage talking, then I place my desks into rows that are all facing the board in the front of the room. Some teachers never realize that their classrooms are just not set up to foster the kind of behaviors they want from their students and that a simple adjustment to the space could do wonders.

Beyond the configuration of your desks, consider any other physical elements of your classroom that could encourage (or, conversely, discourage) proper student behavior. For example, I strategically place the tissue box and electric pencil sharpener near my desk. This setup deters the students who just use those items as a way to be seen by the class or to avoid doing work. Most students do not want to approach my desk multiple times in one class period if they do not genuinely need those items. Also, no matter what configuration I arrange the desks in (rows or circles), I always make sure to have an isolation desk ready in order to keep from having to stop the lesson and make one if someone misbehaves. Remember, creative lesson planning it is not just about the lessons themselves, but about what behaviors you are trying to encourage during each lesson.

Be an Unavoidable Presence

Remember that you and your position in the classroom are also a part of the physical setup that can influence your students' behaviors. Pay close attention to where you will be positioned during each lesson. I strongly recommend that you find strategies and tools that help you keep your eyes on your students as much as possible. Many teachers make the mistake of spending too much time writing on the board with their backs to the class. This is a novice mistake—don't make it!

There are a number of strategies you can take to keep from turning your back to your students. For example, I like to create PowerPoints for each of my lessons instead of writing on the board. I even invested in an electric clicker so that I can change slides without having to be near my computer, giving me the opportunity to walk freely around the classroom as I am explaining the lesson. If PowerPoint isn't your thing, try writing on the board before class, have a student write notes on the board for you, or use a Mobi board to give your instructions. There are many different devices that have been developed that allow teachers to put information on the board without having to physically stand there while students are in the room. Remember that every minute your eyes are not on the class is a minute too long!

Similarly, your own visibility to your students is a vital part of a good discipline plan. Avoid sitting at your desk for long periods of time. When students realize that you are going to stay at your desk, it gives them the opportunity to misbehave because they feel that their behaviors are likely to go unnoticed. Many students want to sit in the back of the room because they believe that teachers rarely venture back there. In your classroom, no seat should feel "safe" from your watchful eyes. Walk around during most of the class period. If you have papers to grade or email to check, sit in an empty student desk among the children. You also may want to put a table or desk in the back of the classroom. The point is to change your physical position to maximize your visibility. It will also catch the students off guard and deter behavior problems. You want to make sure that you are proactive instead of reactive in as many classroom situations as possible. Your goal is to prevent classroom disruptions by being present and aware of what is going on in the classroom.

Make Lessons Meaningful

Students are more willing to take your assignments seriously when you assign context and purpose to them. I have often been asked, "Why do we have to do this?" If you get this question, avoid the temptation to say, "Because I said so." Instead, when I am in this situation, I often pause the lesson and pose the same question to the class: "Why do *you* think we are doing this assignment?" Usually there are several students in the room who can help offer clarity as to why the assignment is important.

If no students are aware of the purpose, I stop and explain it to them. I am honest with my students. Sometimes I tell them that we are required to do this lesson or activity because it will be on the county or state test, but most of the time the lesson has some practical value. It is worthwhile to talk to your students about the purpose of their assignments. Students are more willing to work when they feel that an assignment has a purpose. Try to avoid giving out worksheets or busy work. Teachers who give out meaningless assignments often encounter more behavior problems.

Build Community

Building a sense of community and closeness among your students is a key component of good classroom management. You want to foster an environment where every child feels comfortable to learn and to be themselves. One way to help students develop respectful relationships and feel comfortable with each other is to plan collaborative activities as part of your lessons. Here are some of my go-to community-building activities.

Group Work

A tried-and-true favorite, group work is at the heart of classroom community-building. It gets students engaged in the learning process together and helps them see the value in each others' ideas. It also gives students who are shy an opportunity to share their thoughts and opinions in a much less intimidating setting. Small group activities may still be scary for them, but it will eventually help them become a more integral and active part of the class— because no one in the room should feel like an island.

To make group work successful, be mindful of your students and what you think they can handle. Depending on the dynamics of your class, you may find that letting them choose their own groups is the best way to foster community; other classes may benefit from having you assign the groups, taking into account which personalities will work best together. Or you may want to try both approaches; allowing for some student choice and some teacher selection can cause different leaders to emerge. It's okay to play around with the configurations of the groups to see which ones work best for your desired goals and unique classroom dynamics.

Partner Work

Slightly different from group work, partner work can allow students to develop closer bonds with each other, and it puts even more emphasis on everyone having a voice about the lesson. It is nearly impossible to get away with not speaking in partner work. If you notice a partnership having trouble, join them briefly and ask them questions to help get them started, but don't linger to mediate. You want them to figure out how to work together. It often helps with partner work to have an assignment they are working on to hand in together.

Don't change up partner work too often. It takes time for students to develop relationships with one another. If you want to make sure they are getting more perspectives than just their partners', you can always partner the partners. By this I mean let students talk for a while with their individual partners, but then join partnerships together to form groups of four. Or you can try what I call "speed dating" for education.

For this fun approach to partner work, set up your "speed dating" activity by lining up the desks in two rows facing each other, or put the desks in two circles, with a smaller inner circle facing a larger outer circle. Have your students sit across from each other and share their ideas with their partner for a brief, preset time. When the timer goes off, the students rotate to the next desk, like in speed dating, and begin discussing a new topic or question. This approach to group work is fun and involves lots of movement, so it is great for classes with high-energy students.

Presentations

Most students, if given the option, will never want to speak in front of the class. It is a tough thing to do, for anyone at any age. But teaching students how to have the courage to talk in front of their peers is an invaluable life lesson, and it can lead to some inspiring community-building.

The key is to teach students how to be supportive of each other when taking on this scary task. Show them how to build each other up, how to make the space welcoming and accepting, and then celebrate together after each student has accomplished this challenging task. Don't be afraid to talk openly about how difficult this kind of assignment is. Tell your students about times when you got nervous speaking in front of your peers, and help them reflect on what was so difficult about it once they have all presented. Give them practice by having them make multiple presentations throughout the year.

If you have a class that finds presentations particularly challenging, you can help them practice by allowing them to try out their presentations in small groups before presenting in front of everyone. Or you can allow them to actually make presentations as groups, since it can often be easier for students if they have a few peers with them at the front of the class. Just be sure to require that everyone in the group speak in order to receive credit for the assignment.

It can be difficult for students in the audience to stay focused during presentations. To practice good listening skills, make it a part of their grade for the assignment to write down an interesting point from each of the presentations. Or take a few minutes after each student presents to have everyone in the class write some positive feedback about the presentation. Tell them that you will be taking up this feedback to see how closely they were listening to their peers, and then compile and distribute the feedback to each presenter so that they can see how their peers responded to their presentation.

Peer Review

Whenever you do a writing assignment or presentation, incorporate some kind of element of peer feedback. When completing an assignment, have students edit each other's papers using a rubric. The rubric gives the students the guidance to pay attention to certain aspects of the assignment. It is important to show students that their teacher is not the only source of help and support in the classroom. While doing a student-led feedback assignment, do not allow students to refer back to you for answers or help. Encourage them to trust their partners as well as their own instincts. Many students have the mindset that the teacher is the only one who can determine if an answer is right or wrong. The goal is to show them that their classmates' opinions and knowledge are valuable also. This not only helps students feel that their opinions are valuable, but it also creates a sense of learning as a community.

Competitions

Also try doing class competitions where students are competing against other classes for the best average on a test or for the most classroom participation. Students that feel a sense of classroom community are less likely to act out. When they do misbehave, they may see that their behaviors are not only having a negative effect on their learning, but also letting down the whole class. When a child misbehaves in class and it causes a classroom disturbance, I am quick to point out the fact that they are disrupting the learning of their classmates and friends as well. In the same manner, once students develop a sense of community, they often encourage the defiant students to get back on track. They do not want to see their classmate get in trouble or fall behind the rest of the group.

Always Have a Backup Plan

How quickly are you able to regroup after you realize that a lesson is not working? Do you carry the whole lesson through while it continues to crash and burn? Do you stop the activity immediately and move on to plan B? How many teachers actually have a plan B?

My hope is that every teacher creates at least one backup plan for every lesson, but the reality is that most do not—to the detriment of their classroom management. Not having a backup lesson can become a nightmare if the initial lesson is not working. It is important that while creating a lesson, especially one that is hands-on, you come up with at least one backup plan, just in case.

Often as educators we get excited about lessons that other teachers have shared with us or cool activities that we find online. Many times when colleagues share their lessons, they are completely positive about how amazing these lessons are, but the reality is that they don't always go as planned. That's why you should always have a backup plan. Plan B helps to keep the class under control once you realize that plan A is no longer working. I do not like to try new lessons without having a reliable, tried-and-true lesson ready, just in case. Always plan to have an alternate assignment or a way to adapt the material if students do not seem to be buying in. Teachers who do not have a backup plan will deal with a large array of problems once the children are no longer engaged in the activity.

Strategy #5:

Take Care of Yourself

It is critical that you take care of yourself. You cannot run your classroom well if you are not making sure that *you* are well. You will find that you are more irritable when you have not been getting the proper amount of rest or eating right. Teaching is about more than the "perfect" lesson plans or well-mannered students. A critical component of a successfully run classroom is a teacher who is happy and well-balanced. Everything will seem much easier if you are taking proper care of yourself. So often as new teachers, it is difficult to understand when and how to take care of yourself. New teachers often spend several years stressed and overwhelmed before they realize the importance of taking a break. Be sure to make time for yourself. Take days off. You will be happy you did.

Manage Your Time

Time at Work

If you want to be an effective teacher, you will have to learn to manage your time. Time is a critical part of your teaching day. From the minute your alarm clock wakes you up in the morning to the time you go to bed at night, your day will be governed by time and the way you choose to use it. In order to take good care of yourself, create a schedule for your weekdays. Setting a routine will help you to be more productive and stay on track. Start by setting a time for you to wake up and to go to sleep. Putting yourself on a set schedule will help your body get the proper amount of rest.

After setting up a sleep routine, think about your school day. Where can you streamline some additional routines? Are you a morning or evening person? I like to get to work at least 45 minutes to an hour before my students arrive. I use this time to check emails, grade papers, or prepare for my lesson. Early in the morning, the building is quiet and there are very few teachers in the building to distract me. I like to put in my extra hours in the morning so that

I can leave work as soon as my students leave. This gives me more time in the afternoon to myself. However, if you are more of an evening person, you may find that staying after school works better for you. Just decide whether you want to use the morning or the afternoon as your extra planning time. Avoid using both. Teachers who spend too much time at work will begin to experience burnout and feel more unappreciated.

Other important times to make part of your scheduled routine are restroom breaks. It may seem strange to set specific times to go to the bathroom, but as educators, we have a very unique situation. Unlike other professions, we are not able to go to the restroom whenever the mood hits us. Consider setting mental restroom break reminders for yourself. Try to get your body on a routine so that you are not having to leave your classroom while students are in the room. Of course, you will always need to ask another teacher to watch your class if an emergency arises, but try to avoid having another teacher monitoring as the primary option. Regulating your restroom breaks is important because it will allow you to focus on the lesson while in class and help you to avoid the health problems that come along with waiting too long to use the restroom.

Time for Yourself

Most teachers get into the profession because they love children and want to help them succeed. Because they are so dedicated, they often spend countless hours planning lessons, working late, coming in early, and grading papers. You must be careful not to allow the profession to consume you. Teaching is like eating a powdered doughnut. No matter how hard you try, you are going to still have sugar left behind. The sugar may be on your face, shirt, or hands, but no matter what, it will still be there. Being an educator is very similar. No matter how hard you work at school you will inevitably have something else that needs to be done at home. There are just not enough hours in a day to complete all that is required. However, the important thing is to remember to find the balance. Maximize your time in the building and make the most of your time outside the building. For example, as I stated before, I like to arrive early. This allows me time to prepare for my day. Leaving after bus call gives me time to enjoy my evening. I also choose at least two nights in the week when I am not going to bring my computer home. Those nights I use as no-schoolwork nights, freeing me up to enjoy my evenings doing something fun. Giving yourself set breaks will help you make it through the week. In order to be healthy, you need some down time.

Don't be afraid to take a day off. Some teachers become fatigued and lethargic because they are sitting around waiting for the next school-scheduled break. Don't be afraid to take a "mental health" day. Put some lesson plans together and take a personal day. Play hooky from school and do something fun or catch up on your rest. You will return to work refreshed and ready to start again. Weekends can offer the same rejuvenation. Be careful not to pack too much into a weekend or you will not feel as though you have had a break. I always try to carve out one afternoon or evening for school work and use the rest of the time to relax or take care of errands. School breaks and holidays will give you another opportunity for relaxation. I have found that planning a vacation gives me something to look forward to. It's like giving yourself a reward for all your hard work. Remember that the teacher is a large part of the classroom discipline puzzle. It is important that you are at your very best so that you can properly maintain your classroom. Keeping yourself in a healthy and happy place will help you have energy to foster the best learning environment possible.

Get your Finances in Order

A big stressor for most people is their finances. Since being a new teacher is stressful enough, you want to make sure that you manage the other possible stress contributors in your life. One of the sad truths about education is that teachers are grossly underpaid. Because of this, teachers must be careful to make sound financial decisions. Be sure to live within your means. Your teacher salary can support you, but that will only happen if you are spending wisely.

If you enjoy spending money or you are like most of us and feel the need for more, consider getting a part time job. I know many teachers who have decided to start a small business or take up a part-time job in order increase cash flow. Also, consider using your teaching gifts to make additional money. Start tutoring, sign up for summer school, or do an afternoon program. There are plenty of ways to make additional money. The goal is just to ensure that finances do not become an added concern.

Get Your House in Order

Yes, everyone has his or her own definition of clean, but it is important to make sure that your living space is clean and in order. You will find that during the school year you have very little time for cooking and cleaning. The early years of learning the profession may send your normal household routine into a tailspin. It will be okay. Try to develop a new system for house cleaning. I try to keep my room clean along with the kitchen and all the bathrooms. I am a Language Arts teacher, so once I start grading essays there are often times when the rest of the house becomes neglected. Be patient with yourself.

Forgive yourself for not having time to get everything done. Be selfish sometimes and allow yourself to get some rest instead of cooking and cleaning during your free moments. It may seem that household chores have nothing to do with classroom management, but remember that whatever stresses you will affect your work performance and your overall demeanor.

Set Goals

Education is a profession that provides a lot of opportunities for advancement or change. Many teachers choose to go back to school to receive advanced degrees or add certifications to their certificates. Some teachers choose to change subjects or grade levels. Part of being an educator is understanding the importance of setting goals not only for your students, but also for yourself. Begin to think: Where do I see myself professionally in five years? What do I enjoy about my current position? What would I like to change in the future? Questions like these will help you begin the process of setting professional goals for yourself.

"Teachers who are happy with their position will be more likely to spread that sincere joy to their students."

You will find that by having goals, you are more fulfilled. The job goes beyond the day-to-day routine and becomes steps toward a better tomorrow. Create a plan that will benefit you while also helping you better serve your school and community. Teachers who are happy with their position will be more likely to spread that sincere joy to their students. I even share some of my goals with my students. It is important for them to see that goal-setting is not just for children; it is for anyone who wants to learn and grow.

Setting realistic and obtainable goals will help you also have longevity in the profession. I have heard many teachers say, "I don't know if I can do this for the next 30 years." The reality is that it will be very difficult to stay in the exact same place for the next three decades, but imagine how your career journey would evolve if you changed things up. Try going back to school. Increasing your knowledge will help you regain excitement about being in the classroom. Try changing grade levels. Staying on your toes with new content and a different age group will keep you from the monotony of the same experiences each year. I *can* imagine 30 years of exploring the many facets of education. Don't allow a complacent spirit to step in. Always move forward and look to the next experience.

"It's the Stars for Which We Reach"

The day before my very first education specialist course, I received an email from my professor telling us to create a unique way to introduce ourselves to the group. I wrote this poem and read it on the first night of class.

Born into a home with love overgrown.

An only child very meek and mild.

My mother taught elementary.

My father's goal the same but much higher.

K-12 in a school I knew so well.

Somehow my future sent me back.

Now in the place that inspired me ready

to inspire others.

Two years in.

Where do I begin?

Created two yearbooks. Taught two classes.

No help from the masses.

Still aspiring to prove that, "Every child can learn."

A chant I play in my head at every turn.

My dreams are no longer for me but for the children I teach.

The sky is no longer the limit, but it's the stars for which we reach.

My mind is filled with new ideas and dreams of future careers.

What can I do?

How can I make a difference?

My heart is heavy. My mind is clear.

Can I become a better teacher leader in a year?

My journey has just begun. It will never truly end.

Teaching and learning...

So I'll bring my creativity and pack my humor too.

Because I'm ready for the next phase of this journey.

Are you?

Epilogue

The goal of this book is to leave you in a space where you feel more confident in the teaching journey that is ahead of you. My hope is that in reading my stories, you were able to think back on some of the experiences you had as a student and possibly as a new teacher yourself. I hope that you were not only entertained by my memories and commentary, but also inspired. The purpose of this book is to empower you with the understanding that the ability to be a great teacher is already in you. You are capable of doing awesome things. You are capable of creating an environment where students will not just learn but thrive.

You have done the first step by picking up this book and reflecting on the kind of teacher you want to be. The next step is to put it into practice. Don't try too much at one time. Pick a strategy and work on it for a while. Once you feel comfortable with one, then you can add more. I believe that every great teacher has some crazy stories to tell, so when the outrageous happens, just know that it will make a great story one day. Here are some parting tips for you. Good luck, friend. I'm sure you will inspire and be inspired.

> "The ability to be a great teacher is already in you."

Tips to Live By

✓ *Don't waste your time making a seating chart the first week of school. You have so many things to do, and you will end up making another one anyway once you get to know your students.*

✓ *Avoid negative and cynical people like the plague. You have just started in this profession, and they will bring down your spirit.*

✓ *Never spend more than $30 dollars a month on school supplies, school-related materials, or treats. Most students will not appreciate it, and you will end up needing that money later.*

✓ *Smile even when you don't want to. It helps the day go by faster.*

✓ *Always take attendance at the beginning of class; otherwise, you will forget.*

✓ *Never allow more than one student to leave the room at a time. If it is a bathroom emergency, encourage the next student to wait until the first one returns.*

✓ *Don't volunteer for too much your first year. Being a teacher will be hard enough. (Trust me. I did the yearbook my first two years of teaching.)*

✓ *Stay on top of checking your email. If you fall behind, you will never catch up.*

✓ *Keep drawers and shelves in your classroom. It should appear that things are in order. A messy desk is the first indication that you are losing it.*

✓ *Keep band-aids and hand sanitizer in the classroom. It will eliminate some students need to go to the clinic during class time.*

✓ *Try to fly under the radar. Do not complain to administration about small problems. Wait until it is an issue that truly matters to you.*

✓ *Bring your own lunch and snacks to school. There is nothing worse than a hangry (hungry/angry) teacher.*

✓ *Keep sharpened pencils and a stack of notebook paper in your room. There are bigger battles to fight.*

✓ *Try to speak to every child, every day.*

✓ *When you begin to feel defeated, take a day off. There is nothing wrong with a break.*

✓ *Have students put their bookbags away. Seriously, I had a friend break a toe!*

✓ *Always keep your classroom cold. It keeps students awake and cuts down on germs.*

✓ *Try to complete your lesson plans for the following week on Fridays. This gives you the weekend for grading and recuperating.*

✓ *Always have your students clean up at the end of the day. Custodians are not maids.*

✓ *Arrive to work early. It will give you time to prepare for the day and make any last-minute changes.*

✓ *Remember that every assignment you give does not have to be graded.*

✓ *Always allow wait time before giving your students the answer to a question you have posed. Sometimes they just need time to think.*

Alisa L. Swain is currently a Language Arts teacher in the Georgia public school setting. At this moment, she is finishing her seventh year in the classroom. Alisa holds a Bachelor of Arts in English as well as two education degrees, a Master of Arts in Teaching and a Specialist Degree in Curriculum and Instruction. Alisa's educational background and teaching experiences have proven to her that there is still a need to advocate for and support new teachers. She wrote this book for teachers who are just entering the profession whether it be through career change or straight from college. The goal is to prepare teachers for the discipline challenges they will face and arm them with strategies that will help them confidently maintain control of their classroom environment.